From Emptied to Encouraged

From Emptied to Encouraged

SIERRA RIMES

PALMETTO
PUBLISHING
Charleston, SC
www.PalmettoPublishing.com

© 2024 by Sierra Rimes

All rights reserved
No portion of this book may be reproduced, stored in a retrieval system, or transmitted in any form by any means—electronic, mechanical, photocopy, recording, or other—except for brief quotations in printed reviews, without prior permission of the author.

Paperback ISBN: 979-8-8229-3510-5

Contents

Introduction 1

Chapter 1
American "Idols" 4

Chapter 2
You've Got a Friend in Me 14

Chapter 3
Following the Leader 25

Chapter 4
Accountability 47

Chapter 5
Obedience Isn't Optional 56

Chapter 6
Spot the Difference 115

Chapter 7
The Struggle Is Real 143

About the Author: 161

For the grace of God has been revealed, bringing salvation to all people. And we are instructed to turn from godless living and sinful pleasures. We should live in this evil world with wisdom, righteousness, and devotion to God, while we look forward with hope to that wonderful day when the glory of our great God and Savior, Jesus Christ, will be revealed.

—*Titus 2:11–13 (NLT)*

Introduction

Before you begin reading this book, I want you do to something for me. It's nothing strenuous or tedious, just a simple task that requires very little to no effort. Simply breathe. I'm serious. All I'm asking is that you take a deep breath in. Now, let it out. Very good. Let's continue, shall we?

No matter where you are, you are breathing while reading these words on this page. There is no doubt in my mind that you are alive. That, my friend, is called living. Doesn't it feel good? Living may look different depending on each person. For example, some people may go numerous places that capture the essence of beauty and seek out adventure and thrilling opportunities that can lead them to an exciting life. Others may prefer working a job that they love, coming home from a long day and spending time with their loved ones, or just simply lying on the couch, snuggled up with a cup of coffee. This, too, can offer a fun-filled life. Maybe you are that person who is struggling to breathe. You seem to only get fixated on the loneliness of life and the struggles that come with it. Perhaps it is a chore just to get out of bed in the morning and start the day while you are battling the feeling of depression and emptiness. Trust me when I say I've been there, and I will share more of my story as we move on. Whatever your definition, though, living is an option. You get to choose how you want to live your own life every single day.

Personally, I believe that the only way to truly live is to have Christ in your heart. Now, I know that this is only the introduction, but stay with me. For me, once I accepted Jesus as my Lord and Savior, I began to see the world in a different light. No matter what I am faced with, I know that I have joy, even in the hardships. When things don't turn out my way or seem hopeless at the time, I fully trust and know that I can live a life worth living all because of Jesus. Every breath I take reminds me that I am created for a purpose. Sometimes things may look bleak, and the difficulties may seem heavy, but although I am faced with certain struggles and challenges, I still have joy because I have Christ in my life. Think about a roller coaster. To me, that is exactly how life can look. Take a second and picture it. There are ups when you are joyous and excited, downs when you feel defeated and alone, spins and twists where you may seem stressed and overwhelmed, and sudden drops and plateaus where life can shake you to your core. Amid all my heartache and strife, however, I am confident that I can conquer whatever life throws at me. That is what keeps me living my life to the fullest. One day at a time, knowing that I only have one life to live and God made it especially for me. And guess what? He did the same thing for you too!

Reading has never been one of my strong suits. Though I have always loved to write! When God placed it on my heart to begin writing this book four years ago, I had no idea where it would end up. I knew I really wanted to write on something that hopefully would inspire both the older generation and the ones to come. Then the word "encouragement" came to mind. Something that I think everyone needs a little more of nowadays. Let's face it. This world can be difficult, and life can take you for a spin at a moment's notice. With that being said, it is evident that we all could use some encouragement in our day-to-day lives.

The title, *From Emptied to Encouraged*, is exactly what I want you to be after reading this book, and I pray that it becomes a reality. I want you to feel encouraged and motivated to take on anything this world will throw at you. I want you to become a better you! I will share personal stories from my life that have both helped and hindered me in my walk with the Lord. I wanted to share pieces of my story to hopefully encourage and uplift you on your own life journey. I prayerfully sought out each section and kept you in mind while writing. There are subpoints in each chapter so you can read at your own pace. Keep in mind, this book is considered to be a challenge for you. I don't want you to read it and forget what you have read, but internalize it. When reading it, ask yourself the tough questions that will make you become a better person. To help, I have provided some thought-provoking questions for you to think upon at the end of each section. This isn't considered to be homework but will help you to reflect and personalize it into your own life so that you can be changed for the better. I pray that the words on these pages will not only show you how God helped me throughout my life but also motivate you to draw closer to God and rely on Him despite anything you might face.

Chapter 1
American "Idols"

Those who cling to worthless idols turn away from God's love for them.
—*Jonah 2:8 (NIV)*

I've grown up watching the show *American Idol* since I was a young girl in elementary school. My mom, granny, and I would be curled up in the living room ready to co-judge the contestants along with the real judges, Simon, Randy, and Paula. If you have never seen the show, it is a contest to see who can sing the best. Celebrities like Carrie Underwood, Kelly Clarkson, and Clay Aiken have all entered the spotlight by showing off their talent of singing on this one-of-a-kind TV hit.

This show is called *American Idol*, I think, simply because of what the contestants go through. America votes and chooses someone to be a representation of an idol that people can look up to in their lives. Of course, they are chosen because of their singing ability also. Contestants from around the globe audition for this show, and only a select few make it to the finals, then the finale. Once the person is chosen to be the next American Idol, they are in the public eye for life. All eyes are on them. No longer is

Carrie Underwood just a girl from the country, but a public figure that girls and adults of all ages can look up to and admire.

In the dictionary, the word *idol* has two meanings. One is an image or representation of an object to worship a god. The other is a person or thing that you greatly admire and love. Basically, an idol is something that takes the place of the one true God, Jesus Christ, in your life.

Is there something in your life that, if God wanted to take it away, you would cling to it tighter? That thing or person, my friends, is considered an idol in your life. Whether it is a sport, a hobby, a relationship (boyfriend/girlfriend, family member, friend), the internet (Facebook, Instagram, Twitter), or even a cell phone, these idols can have a significant effect on you, your relationships, and most importantly, your relationship with God.

If these things are affecting your relationships, you need to do some evaluating. You prioritize your time based on your desires. If you love to dance, you dance like no one is watching. If you like to play an instrument, you practice it until your fingers are sore. I guess what I'm getting at is that we all have the same twenty-four-hour days. The question is, how are you spending it?

I admit that sometimes, when I got home from a day at school, I would sit on the couch and take (what seemed like) a minute to scroll social media to see what was happening. Little did I know, I wasted about thirty minutes mindlessly scrolling the internet when I could have been doing something productive that actually mattered. How about you? We need to crave the Word of the Lord rather than the material things He created.

The Key to Happiness

Back when I was young, I believed in Santa Claus. I remember going to the shops as a young child and getting to take pictures with Santa while telling him what I wanted for Christmas that year. My mom and I would wait in long lines at the local mall so I could sit on his lap. Each year, my cousins and I were so excited to write a list to Santa, put out milk and cookies the night before his arrival, and hopefully stay up late enough to see him coming down the chimney with a bag full of toys. Somehow, though, we always managed to fall asleep.

I remember that my stepdad wanted to buy me a house key one year. So a couple days before Christmas, he went to the local department store and had a key made that could unlock my home. Seeing that the key had Winnie the Pooh, which I loved, he purchased the key and quickly wrapped it up when he got home. When I opened it Christmas morning, it was like I had won the lottery! All of my mom's presents that she had spent time and money on were tossed to the side. Honestly, I think I cried, I was so happy knowing that I had gotten a house key. It made me feel so grown-up. Ridiculous, I know. Who would have thought that such a small thing would make me so happy?

After opening the gift, I immediately went down to my cousins' house, which was next door, and showed both of them the key. Of course I had to lock the door as I left to ensure that the key worked. I was beyond thrilled!

When school was back in session, all of my friends told about their treasures Santa had left them. Some got the latest video games or Barbie dolls, but I got a house key! Needless to say, that was the best Christmas present I had gotten that year. As you can probably tell, it doesn't take a lot to get me excited.

A couple of weeks went by, and I was still excited to rush up the stairs and unlock the door every time I came home from school. Days turned into weeks, weeks turned into months, and months turned into years. With each passing day, the excitement of the house key soon faded. No longer did I enjoy using the key. I was just eager to get inside from a long day at school.

Like my twelve-year-old self, maybe you are excited about something that was given to you or that you had purchased. This object could help you become more confident, more social, or more independent. While those are all fine and good, it will provide joy only for a season. No one can purchase true happiness no matter how hard they try. In due time, the object will leave you as empty as you were before you had it—providing only temporary happiness.

I just mentioned that you can't buy or purchase happiness. There is no object that you can buy that will fully sustain you. Yes, it may provide happiness for a season, just like my house key, yet in the long run, it will leave you wanting more of the next best thing that comes along. God is not concerned about your happiness as much as He is with your holiness. True happiness depends on your holiness to the Lord. Nothing else. You will never be fully satisfied until you give your life to Jesus. If you are pleasing Him and doing what He has called you to do, you are going to be the happiest you have ever felt! And that, my friends, is a promise.

Physical Idols

Throughout high school, I had about five close friends. It seemed like we did everything together. We went to dinner together, had bowling trips, and slept over at one another's houses. Now, we weren't necessarily the popular kids, but we seemed to befriend everyone that came along. The five of us could be very goofy yet knew when heart-to-hearts needed to happen. We were inseparable! Since the five of us were busy hanging out almost every weekend, none of us truly realized the reality to come…graduation.

I would like to say that nothing changed after getting a high school diploma and that we are all as close as we once were; however, that is far from the truth. Upon graduating, I still thought that we would hang out just like we used to and everything would go back to normal. When graduation came and went, no longer were my weekends devoted to my friends. My life soon was filled with job interviews and college scholarship applications—trying to move on from the past and focus on the future.

I had found my happiness through my friends. That is what sustained me. Whenever I went to school, I would always seek them out first. I talked with them about pretty much anything and everything, relying on them for my happiness instead of God. Since I idolized my friends so much, the Lord took them away. Now, I'm not saying that God plopped down and physically moved them out of my life, but we no longer talked or spent time together like we used to. Some of my friends got married, others had children right off, and I was starting college. I'm not saying any of these things are bad. We all just took different paths in life.

God is not a God that is looking down from Heaven wanting to disrupt your life. Saying that God doesn't want you to be happy simply isn't true. Don't get me wrong; having friends is a great thing. It is one of the many ways that God has blessed me. I truly believe that the Lord wants us to enjoy most of the things on this earth because He has created them. Notice how I said *most* of the things on this earth. He wants you to have the best life you can, but that does come with boundaries and stipulations. God wants us to live our lives to the fullest. He wants you to dream big and to have a life worth living! You were created for His glory and not your own wants and desires. Ultimately, your happiness won't go far unless it is driven by the Lord. A wise heart doesn't get overly attached to the things of God, but only to God. The Bible says that God is a jealous God in Exodus 20:4. He doesn't want anyone or anything to come between your relationship with Him. When something or someone does get in the way, you better be ready for the Lord to remove it from your life.

Role Models vs. Idols

Let's get something straight. There is a distinct difference between a role model and an idol. I previously defined the word *idol*. Now let's dig deeper into the word *role model*. A role model is someone that is looked at by others to imitate. So, who do you want to be like in life? Maybe you want to be a great cook like your grandmother. Some of you might want to be a famous singer like Reba McEntire or Carrie Underwood. Maybe you just want to be strong and independent like one of the members in your family. Whatever the case, why do you want to be like them?

Don't get me wrong: being a celebrity like Reba or Carrie does have its perks; however, being famous isn't the only reason you should want to be like someone. In your own life, think about why you want to be like that certain person. Why do you want to emulate them? I believe that you should search the heart of the person and identify their values. Are they a believer who loves God? Are they a loving and caring person? Do they look for the best in other people? Do they help you become a better you? If you answered no to any of these questions, I challenge you to reevaluate the role models in your life.

Although there are people in this world that try their best to reflect the best qualities possible, because they are human they will slip up and make mistakes. Just like me and you, we all have our flaws. However, God is not a God who makes mistakes. He is perfect in every way (see Psalm 18:30). In Genesis 3, the first humans ever, Adam and Eve, sinned against God. They did the opposite of what the Lord told them to, therefore sinning (making bad decisions that can lead to eternal consequences). Ever since then, humans are going to fall short. There is no denying that. We all sin on a daily basis. We all do things that we aren't proud of. As you go through life, people are going to let you down, broken promises are going to be made, and the trust that you have built can be broken in an instant. With that being said, why put your faith or trust in someone that will fail you regularly? I encourage you to put your faith and trust in someone who will never fall short, Jesus Christ. God encourages all of us to seek Him, and in turn, we will become better people because of it.

Are there any idols in your life? If so, what are they?

Why do you think that you have made these things idols?

What steps can you take to release them from your life?

What can you do to make God your first priority?

Are You Loud and Proud?

In the Bible, there is a story about Jesus being tempted by the enemy, Satan (See Matthew 4:1–11, Luke 4:1–13, and Mark 1:9–13). Within this story, Jesus is being tried by the enemy. Satan is trying to get Jesus to jump off the highest point of the building. Why would Satan ask this of Jesus? I believe that Satan wanted to test God in a way that made Him prideful. Jesus could have said, "You already know that I am Jesus—I can do no wrong." Yet He didn't. Jesus knew He was being tempted and refused to relent to Satan's request.

When a person is prideful, he or she is feeling satisfied with what they have achieved. They want people to admire them because of their achievements. Every person on this Earth is unique and special in the Lord's eyes. Because of this, God created you with the talents and abilities to be successful (whatever your definition of successful is). With that being said, no one should be arrogant with what they have achieved, because it is all from the Lord. He has gifted you with the skills to do it and to do it well. Don't get me wrong; you should want to be proud of all of your accomplishments, and you should always be confident and secure in yourself. However, when you are becoming arrogant and narcissistic, then it becomes an issue. People sometimes do what they think is right in their own eyes, but God has given us the skills and tools to accomplish each new task. You did nothing on your own. Give credit where credit is due. Therefore, we should all be grateful to God that He has provided us with wonderful gifts, talents, and specialties; ergo, be humble.

God opposes the proud, but gives grace to the humble.

—*James 4:6 (NLT)*

When I was in my early twenties, I applied to work at a Christian camp in North Carolina called Snowbird Wilderness Outfitters. My youth pastor had been taking groups of students to this camp every summer since I can remember, so I thought I would apply to work on staff (I'll talk more about camp in a later chapter). So I sat down at the computer and began working. I quickly discovered that this wasn't going to be something I could do in one night. The fifty-question application was so tedious and in-depth. To add to the severity of the job, each response could be no less than five hundred words. The questions could range from "What is your testimony?" (basically, how did you come to have a relationship with Jesus?) to "Why do you believe that the Bible is 100 percent true?" It really made me test my faith as a Christian.

I became a believer when I was in middle school. My mom always took me to church every time the doors were opened. So by growing up in the faith, I thought I knew a lot as a believer. I could tell you the answers to all the basic questions; however, there was so much more I needed to learn. Not only to get this job but to understand the true meaning of my belief in Christianity. I admit I was being prideful, thinking I already knew what I needed to in order to "get by" in my Christian faith.

The application process took me about four long months to complete. During those months, my faith was pushed and challenged. It seemed like I would complete one question, and then the list kept growing! I thought I would never get finished. Though each question was difficult and required some soul-searching and scripture-seeking, I was finally able to complete it, get accepted, and grow in my knowledge and faith, all while the Lord was stripping me of my pride at the same time. I did nothing to accomplish this tedious task on my own. The Lord knew what steps I needed to make it happen. He alone provided me with the tools to successfully complete it, and boy...am I grateful!

So, what is my point? Don't let pride get in the way of you and the Lord. Like I mentioned earlier, being prideful isn't something to boast about. Jesus knew that arrogance would have gotten Him nowhere. He knew that if He was conceited and said such things, He would be no better than Satan himself. Don't let the enemy provoke you into becoming bigheaded. Yes, you may be blessed with that big promotion, the fancy car, or the spouse and kids you have longed for, but that doesn't mean you have to put others down and flaunt what you have. Be grateful to the Lord for His many blessings upon your life by showing humility.

Do you consider yourself a humble person? Why or why not?

If not, what can you do to show humility in your own life?

Chapter 2
You've Got a Friend in Me

There is a friend who sticks closer than a brother.

—*Proverbs 18:24 (NIV)*

No matter what stage of life you are in, I'm sure you can think of one person that you've met who is now your friend. Now, I'm not saying that you and this person have to be close and share your deepest, darkest secrets with each other. But at some point, you both enjoyed something that brought you closer together. Maybe you were in the same class in grade school. Others of you may have met your friends doing extracurricular activities like volleyball, band, or dance. Whatever the case, probably some type of shared experience at one time in your life has led to a wonderful friendship.

The saying goes that friends are easy to find and easy to lose. A true friend, however, is hard to find and even harder to lose. Anyone can be a friend to others. It doesn't take a lot of effort. Friends just come and go throughout your life. Being a true friend, though, is something that everyone should strive to be.

I'm sure we all have acquaintances in our lives. You know, the people you talk to at random times but don't really have a deep connection with. Although friends can be great to have, genuine friends have your back no matter what and don't walk away when things get tough. It seems like they are always there to give a listening ear, a helping hand, and can speak truth into your life even if you don't want to hear it.

Remember, anyone can be a friend to someone, but true friends are something special that you never want to lose. True friendships are a blessing from God and should be treated as such. God puts some people in your life only for a season. Those are regular friendships. True friendships, however, are there for a reason and not just for a season, helping and motivating you throughout your life.

Be a Friend That You Would Want to Have

In the iconic Pixar film *Toy Story*, the ending song is "You've Got a Friend in Me." It states all the things that you would want to have in a friendship. In order for someone to be a good friend to you, you need to exemplify true friendship yourself. Being a friend to someone is a choice; therefore, choose your friends wisely. Be an example of a genuine friend that people want and need.

Take a minute and think about your best friend. What qualities come to mind? What made that friendship stand out from the rest? When choosing your friends, hopefully you wouldn't want someone who lies all the time, is very arrogant and dramatic, or is always trying to tear you down. Instead, find people who are fun, that you enjoy being around, and who can invest in your life for the better. Here are just a few qualities that my friends and I try to emulate in our own friendship. I pray that it helps and grows your friendships with others too.

Be a Listener

Understand this, my dear brothers and sisters: You must all be quick to listen, slow to speak, and slow to get angry. Human anger does not produce the righteousness that God desires.

—*James 1:19–20 (NLT)*

I absolutely love being intentional with people! It is one of my love languages. (If you haven't taken the love language test, I encourage you to do so.) Personally, I love getting to know a person's heart along with helping and motivating them. So on my days off work, I usually will ask one of my friends to have lunch because we really don't see each other that often due to our busy schedules. It's nice when we can get together and catch up with each other while also investing in each other's lives.

On this particular chilly day, my friend and I decided to have lunch at a little restaurant in our hometown. We got to our meeting place, took off our jackets, hung them on the chairs behind us, and then sat down and looked at the menu. When we finally made our selections and the waiter had taken our order, I began the conversation by asking what the Lord was doing in her personal life. She then started sharing about how she was having issues at home, how her job was chaotic, and she felt like she wasn't growing in her relationship with the Lord like she should be. Now, if she had shared all of her problems, worries, and joys with me and then gotten up from the table and left without me saying a word, that would be crazy (and rude)! She didn't take time for me to respond and truly listen to my feedback. Without letting me speak into her life, that wouldn't be a true friendship.

Like the saying goes, relationships are a two-way street. No matter what relationship you are in, you can't grow closer together without communication. You can converse all day long with one another, but unless you actually stop talking and listen (I mean *really* listen) to them, your relationship will not be strong and grow like it should. Don't just listen to respond to people, but listen to understand them. Listen with intent. Remember, you get out of it what you put into it. If you were on the other end of the conversation, I hope that you would want someone to speak into your life. I think that's why God gave us two ears and one mouth for a reason: to listen twice as much as you speak. Be a friend who truly listens to others, making people feel both seen and heard.

Can you say that you truly listen to others?

Be an Encourager

I met one of my closest friends when I worked my first summer at Snowbird in North Carolina. I will call her Ashley. She, too, was working that same summer and ended up being one of my roommates. The first night we met, she hugged me tightly and told me that we were going to be great friends. Now, I didn't know this girl at all. Little did I know that we would form a close friendship, and she would make a great impact in my life back then.

Looking back to that first summer, when Ashley could tell that something was wrong, she would always make a point to check in on me and see how I was doing. She would write notes and scripture verses to me, as well as other staff members (only to girls, of course), to show that she cared about us all individually. The notes weren't long, just impactful enough for each person. Also, no matter how late it was (staff members went to bed really late), before bed each night she made it a point to check on me and see how I was doing, since it was my first summer working there. One morning, I remember sitting on the steps, waiting to go into the church service. Ashley then walked by, put some flowers and a note in my lap, and continued to walk away. She may not have known the significance of her actions, but I still can remember that little gesture several years later. It's the little things that make a huge impact in the lives of others. To this day, Ashley is still one of the most encouraging people I have ever met!

Therefore, encourage one another and build one another up, just as you are doing.

—*1 Thessalonians 5:11 (ESV)*

Although it can be challenging at times, encouraging people is something I strive to do daily. Being an encourager is something that takes time and effort. It just doesn't happen overnight. It mainly starts with a positive mindset. Since this world is filled with craziness, it is easy to get caught up in it and be negative. However, if your mind isn't right, your heart won't be either, making you a pessimist and not very fun to be around. Who wants to be around those types of people? Not me! I want to be around other cheerful and encouraging people, and I hope you do too. Therefore, I pray that you take little steps to becoming one and reflect that light onto others. Here are some things you can do to get started:

- Pray for others. There is so much power in prayer.
- Write scriptural notes or encouraging texts to people.
- Call someone who may need a pat on the back.
- Visit a friend or family member that you haven't seen in a long time.
- Partake in a small gesture that shows someone that you care about them (pick flowers or buy them their favorite snack).

These steps are just five of the many things you can do to hopefully inspire someone in your friend group, family, or community who needs it. Encouragement is contagious. Once you start a chain, you might be surprised how long and far it goes. You might even start a chain reaction! I pray that you succeed and can become an encouragement to others around you.

What are some things you can do to encourage others?

Not only should you encourage others, but you need to be encouraged as well. Everyone does. You can't pour out of an empty cup. Basically, you can't pour out encouragement into people's lives if you are not filled up with it yourself. I wrote this book to hopefully do just that. However, like I mentioned earlier, encouraging people can sometimes be challenging. There are days when I am lazy and can't even get my life together, let alone worry about others and what they are going through. When those days do hit, I usually listen to worship music or a motivational podcast. But the best tool I know to motivate and encourage me is the Bible (God's living and active

Word). There are so many stories in there that are relevant to this day and age. I pray that you, too, not only will read it but can become transformed by it! Let it renew your mind and strengthen your soul. Then, in turn, you can shine a light to others around you with the power that only comes from the Lord.

Describe how you fill your cup.

Be There or Be Square

On the radio, I once heard the phrase, "There is power in your presence." Now, I couldn't fully grasp the whole concept. As I reflected upon it during the day, I started to see how just being there for someone can really show that you care about them individually.

My granddaddy (my mom's dad) and I were very close growing up. I lived right next door to him and my granny, so I saw him pretty much every day. He would usually tease me about my wardrobe, ask me about school and my future career, and try to give me life lessons while working in the yard on weekends. He was always a tough guy on the outside, but inside he was a godly man. My granddaddy had a heart of gold with a ministry mindset to serve others whenever the chance arose. We were like two peas in a pod. So I was both shocked and devastated when he passed away in 2016 of a massive heart attack.

I remember getting the call from my mom. I was working on staff at Snowbird at the time, and I was out with friends, eating at a restaurant after church on a Sunday night. My mom called while trying to hold back tears. I could tell something was wrong. She finally said, "Granddaddy has passed away." I immediately asked what happened, and then she began to explain that he had a massive heart attack a couple minutes before she called. I could feel the tears welling up in my eyes as I sat in the booth along with four of my coworkers.

Being that I am from Florida, it is a long way to and from North Carolina. Since I didn't have any family around me, my mom prayed before calling, asking the Lord to surround me with friends who could comfort me during that tough time. I then told them what had happened, and then we all got in the car and headed back to camp. As I sobbed the whole way back, thinking of my family, my friends who I rode with were all silent. Not asking any questions or trying to lift my spirits, everyone was praying for me, knowing that this was difficult news to hear. When we arrived at the campus, each one said, "We are praying for you and your family." Those eight little words made all the difference.

Sometimes, you don't want to explain why you are mad, angry, frustrated, or hurt. I get that and have experienced it myself. Sometimes all you want is to be left alone. If we are honest, though, that's not what we really want. Yes, some days you want to be alone, and that's okay. But look at the big picture. I know I would want someone to be there for me. How about you? A shoulder to cry on, with ears to listen and open arms just in case we might need embracing, can mean a great deal to someone. Find people in your life who can and will pray over you. To me, that is the greatest source of encouragement. There is power in you being there for someone. You might not know the significance of your presence, but to another person, it can have a meaningful effect on them.

I'm sure we all have those friends in our lives that feel like family. You tell each other secrets that no one else knows, sometimes fight and bicker like siblings, and comfort each other in times of need. I'm sure we all want friends like that (minus the fighting and bickering). But what if I told you that at some point in your life, they will let you down? Would you believe me? I'm sure right now you are thinking that I don't know what I am talking about. *You don't know them like I do. They wouldn't do that. I've known them since I was young.* Congratulations! I'm glad you have friends like that. Let me say that although friends can be a great source of comfort when you need it, only God can fully sustain and comfort you like no one else can.

People are tangible, making them easy to confide in because you can actually see and hear them. You can see the emotions on their faces. You can hear the tone in their voices. You can feel the comfort and love in their hugs and embraces. However, everyone is a sinner. No matter how good of a friend they are, at some point they are going to betray you, hurt you, anger you, or disappoint you, and you are going to do the same thing to them. Why? No one is perfect on this earth. It's inevitable. Just because you can't physically see or touch God doesn't mean He isn't there. God is the ultimate source of comfort and peace in your life when you need it most. When all else fails, turn to Him. He will never leave you nor forsake you (Deuteronomy 31:6–8). Rely on Him and seek Him out. When it seems like no one is there, God always is, ready and waiting for you.

If You Lie Down with Dogs...

Bad company corrupts good character.

—1 Corinthians 15:33 (NLT)

I've always been a dog lover. My family has owned countless dogs over the years, ranging from Beagles to Dachshunds to Labradors. Their sizes, shapes, and colors all differ, along with the dogs' temperaments and moods. Depending on the breed, you might get a hunting dog, a playful pooch, or a timid canine. However, what seems to be the same for all animals, especially dogs, is that they can all get fleas.

Dogs manage to get these creatures on and in their fur, making it hard to see unless they tend to scratch and bite themselves. As the owner, hopefully you try to stop the flea infestation by bathing the dog or getting the dreaded cone of shame. The problem still doesn't go away, though, until all of the animals around them are gone or you begin to take action in making the dog feel better.

Most likely, if dogs were around other dogs at one point in time, fleas will jump from one dog to another. The same can happen to people. Not with fleas, mind you, but with our actions and behaviors. What we do and how we behave can have a significant effect on the people around us and vice versa. Their actions and attitudes can rub off onto us and change who we are. Like the saying goes, if you lie down with dogs, you will get up with fleas. Meaning that whoever you surround yourself with will have either a positive or negative role in your life. Therefore, choose your friendships wisely. The people in your life play a large part in it whether you think so or not. They can influence you, especially in the adolescent years, but only if you let them. I encourage you to hang around and socialize with people that will have a positive influence on you. If you do choose to hang around with certain types of people, as Jesus did, you be the impactful one. After all, Jesus associated with people who were the complete opposite of Him (drunks, prostitutes, and tax collectors), yet He never changed His character to fit in. In the end, those people turned to believers because of Jesus's impact on their lives. So whomever you decide to hang around, make the choice to influence them for the better, especially if you believe in Jesus.

Do you think you are impacting others' lives for the better? If so, how?

Being a Christian, though, isn't always easy or fun. That's why I think a lot of people don't want to surrender their life to Jesus. They think it will take away all the pleasurable things in life. However, it is quite the opposite. Once you become a believer, you are called to live differently than the world. Yes, being a follower of Jesus means it can be challenging. You might have to stand out from the crowd. You may be the odd one out at the table. You might even get talked about behind closed doors, hearing that you are a loser, a dweeb, or a Goody Two-shoes. The reward, though, is so much greater than the ridicule you might receive.

If your friends do something that you don't think is right, move on. Stand up for your faith and stand out from the crowd. Take it from someone who has been there. I promise, God will provide you with godly friendships, but only if you seek and obey Him first and foremost. If you want to make an impact in someone's life, why not make it a good one and be like Jesus?

How can you stand up for your faith?

Chapter 3
Following the Leader

Don't let anyone think less of you because you are young. Be an example to all believers in what you say, in the way you live, in your love, your faith, and your purity.

—*1 Timothy 4:12 (NLT)*

I loved watching the Disney classic *Peter Pan* when I was young. If you have ever seen the movie, there is a scene where John, the Lost Boys, and his brother Michael journey to find the Indians in Neverland. Whatever John does and wherever he goes, the Lost Boys, along with Michael and his stuffed teddy bear, follow right behind him. They stay on the same path that John does, not straying from it. While traveling, they all sing a song called "Following the Leader."

Being that it was John's first trip to Neverland, I am certain that he didn't have any idea where he was going. He just knew that he wanted to see the Indians, and he was going to make it happen whether they got lost or not. That can be true in the real world today. Just look around. People follow others whom they trust. The journey that they lead you on can seem enjoyable until you get to the destination. If you remember from the movie,

John got the Lost Boys and Michael nearer to their destination unharmed; however, once they got closer to the Indians, they got tied up. I'm sure that wasn't John's intention when leading them there. Sadly, though, that was where the journey had ended.

Be a Leader That You Would Want to Follow

There have been many leaders throughout our world. Some have good characteristics of being a leader, but others may not have the necessary leadership skills but are chosen for that particular job anyway. Whether it is your teacher, a boss, or even the president, God puts people in leadership for a purpose. He has ordained them over you for a reason. We may not understand God's reasoning behind it, but I am certain that He knows our future better than we do.

From the time when I was young, my dad has always told me to be a leader and not a follower. A follower goes along with whatever the leader chooses to do and doesn't venture out on their own path. A follower takes orders well yet can sometimes need a confidence boost to do their own thing and be an independent individual. I admit that growing up, I was a follower. I went along with whatever the plans were, and I had a hard time standing up for myself and what I actually wanted. Now, I never got into things like drugs or alcohol. That was where I drew the line. However, I never seemed to be confident enough to branch out and go my own way. I tended to always follow someone else's path.

Since I have matured, I have seen where being a leader rather than a follower can have so many more advantages, though it does take a lot more independence and responsibility. Anyone can be a leader if they choose to be. Nevertheless, there are distinct differences in being known as a leader and being thought of as a great leader.

What defines a great and well-placed leader? You may not know what these leadership skills look like, and that's okay. It took a while before I found out too. No matter your age, there is always room to grow your leadership ability. Like I mentioned earlier, being a leader is a choice, just like anything. Being a great leader, though, is something that you have to work at. It just doesn't come naturally. Now that I am older, I often try to keep certain qualities in mind as I try to become more confident with my own leadership skills. My prayer is that you too will be able to grab hold of these qualities and become the leader that God wants you to be.

Great Leaders Strive to Become the Best They Can Be (For Themselves and for God)

When you are a leader, it seems that everyone is looking up to you and wanting to be like you. No pressure, am I right? As the classic Spider-Man, Peter Parker, put it, "With great power, there must also come great responsibility." We should all want to strive to be the best we can be for ourselves, for our family, and for God. But what if we don't feel ready? What if we feel inadequate and unprepared for what God is calling us to do? Ever been there? I certainly have.

In the book of 1 Samuel, God summons a man named Samuel to choose the next king of Israel. Now, Samuel was a man who loved the Lord and wanted to obey Him no matter the cost. Because of this, the Lord spoke through Samuel in order to choose who the next king would be. He said, "Fill your flask with olive oil and go to Bethlehem. Find a man named Jesse who lives there, for I have selected one of his sons to be my king" (1 Samuel 16:1, NLT).

First off...what an honor! The Lord sought out Samuel to go and choose the next king. Talk about humbling. Samuel didn't like the spotlight or making his presence known. He simply obeyed the Lord without hesitation. So I'm sure he was surprised that the Lord sought him out to do this task.

Surprised or not, Samuel did as the Lord commanded. One by one, Jesse's eight sons came. Samuel tried to pick the person who was the strongest, the bravest, and the most masculine. Yet each one Samuel chose, the Lord declined. By this time, I am sure he was getting more and more frustrated by the second. The Lord then reminded Samuel, "People judge by outward appearance, but the Lord looks at the heart" (1 Samuel 16:7, NLT). Jesse then called for his last son, David, who was a shepherd and the youngest of all his brothers, to see if he would be chosen to be the next king.

Let's stop here for a moment. Do you know what a shepherd does? They watch sheep! Seems like an easy job...at least that was what I thought at first. Being a shepherd was no easy task in those days. Their job was to protect the sheep from wild animals, guard them while they slept, and guide them to food and away from harm. I'll go right out and say it...like any animal, sheep can be hard to handle too. When you're herding them, they tend to go in a lot of different directions, causing the sheepdogs or the shepherds to get them back in formation. (Sound anything like you? Straying from the path?) Anyway...I'd say a shepherd had to be on guard a lot while tending to their flock. Also, back in ancient times, a shepherd was considered unclean. People thought they were outcasts because they dealt with stinky and filthy sheep. This meant that they usually worked alone, just themselves and the sheep for days on end. Talk about lonely.

As we look forward into the story, we see that God does anoint David, a shepherd boy, as king. David didn't question God's intentions as I might have. He just stood there, among his dad and older brothers, as Samuel anointed him. If that were me, I would have been like, *God, you've got the wrong person. I can't do this! I have known shepherding all my life. I know nothing about running a kingdom.* Yet David didn't. God chose David not because he was handsome and brave, but because He saw his heart and knew his intentions. God saw something in David that no one else had. Therefore, God chose Him purposefully, not accidentally. In fact, scripture stated that once David became anointed, the Spirit of the Lord came powerfully upon him. That is exactly what God does when we step out in faith and do what He has called us to do. He empowers and strengthens us to be the best we can be, but only if we let Him. If God has called you to it, He will bring you through it. He has a purpose and plan that only you can fulfill. Don't waste the opportunities He has given you.

Now, David's anointing doesn't mean that all went well for him. This is certainly not the case. Actually, in the next chapter, he fights a giant named Goliath (1 Samuel 17), runs from someone who was trying to kill him (1 Samuel 18–22), and becomes tempted, angry, jealous, and sorrowful. Through all those trials, though, David was considered a man after God's own heart (1 Samuel 13:14). He knew that the Lord was with him through the good and the bad. Once David messed up, he reconciled it and wanted to do better for himself and for God.

David didn't know how his life would play out once he became king of Israel. He didn't know the outcome of the battle against Goliath. He didn't know if he would be killed by Saul, the former king of Israel. But he did know God, and he knew that God would be with him every step of the way. David's fear didn't go away, but his faith grew despite his fear. Although his challenges may have been great, David knew that his God was greater than anything he might face, making it easier to step out in faith. If God was with David, He will be with you too!

Are you having a hard time saying yes to God? Maybe it means starting a new career path or moving to a new place. It might mean standing up for others who are afraid to stand up for themselves. It might be going one way when your friends and family go another direction because of your convictions and beliefs. It might be as simple as just doing the thing that scares you or gives you anxiety. I understand. All of those things can be frightening for one reason or another. Even though it might be challenging, I encourage you to step out of your comfort zone and trust God. Don't question Him, but say yes to Him like David did when he was becoming king. Remember, if you never give God the opportunity to lead your life, you will never see the outcome and abundant blessings He has for you. If we abide in Christ, His desire for us will soon follow.

Is it easy for you to say yes to God?

If not, what makes you question Him?

Great Leaders Serve Others Well

A servant's heart is something that people should strive to have. We should want to serve others. Not only does it help the individual, but it also allows you to feel happiness. In today's society, people can be self-centered. They don't consider other people or their feelings. They are only concerned with pleasing themselves and getting what they want regardless of the other people involved. In the previous chapter, I mentioned some things that will help others show that you care. Well, what better way of showing someone those qualities than by serving them?

Work willingly at whatever you do, as though you were working for the Lord rather than for people.
—Colossians 3:23 (NLT)

Whenever church members get together, there usually is food involved. At the church I attend, every Wednesday night we serve a huge meal to feed children and families that come. The ladies in the kitchen do a fabulous job making the numerous amount of food every Wednesday night. The men usually help with getting everyone drinks and monitoring trash cans as needed. After they have all cooked, served, and cleaned the kitchen, most of them still teach and help the children in their classroom activities. Talk about a servant's heart. These men and women have a heart for ministry. None of them get paid to do what they do every Wednesday night. However, they are leaders who are ready and willing to serve the students and families that pass by in whatever way possible.

Now, you might not be a churchgoer. Therefore, you may be thinking, *I don't go to church, so there is really nothing that I can do to serve others.* That is where you are wrong. You don't have to attend a church to have a ministry mindset. There are numerous opportunities right in your own community and family, but you have to go out and be the one to initiate them. It is up to you. While you serve the people around you, I challenge you to keep these things in mind:

- Serve others willingly. If something needs to be done, do it. Don't be lazy and wait for someone else to do the task. If you wait, it may never get completed. Therefore, you might miss out on an opportunity to invest in someone's life for the better.
- Don't make excuses. Serving others can be challenging sometimes. When you do make excuses for yourself, it will hurt you in the long run and possibly make you have regrets later on.
- Serve others wholeheartedly, not selfishly. Whether the person is your best friend, your worst enemy, or a stranger on the street, you are to help them with a giving and joyful attitude regardless of the person or task involved.
- Go the extra mile to serve someone. Anything that is worth doing is worth doing right. What you put into your service, you will get in return.
- Serve in whatever way possible. I understand that some people can't serve every time the chance arises. When you can, people need to see that you are ready to help them no matter what you may lose. Whatever you have to give up (your time, money, or the clothes off your back), if you are willing and able, don't miss out on the chance to be a blessing to those around you.

Serving others isn't always glamorous or easy to do. It may take a lot of determination and humility. Sometimes, people might not always appreciate what you do for them or recognize your efforts. It just depends on the person and the situation. That may be hard to take in, but don't let those things discourage you from lending a helping hand. Instead, let them motivate you to continue helping for the sake of others.

Also, no matter who you are helping, having the right attitude needs to be taken into consideration. If the person or people whom you serve see that you are doing it with a bad attitude (i.e., grumbling or complaining), he or she will think it isn't genuine. The Bible talks about having a servant's heart. Jesus wants you to put your whole heart into those you serve. He wants us to serve others with a godly and joyful attitude no matter the situation. Then people will be blessed because of it. You are not serving others simply for your own recognition and praise. I love serving others simply because it mimics Jesus's life, and I want to become more like Him. Look for chances to serve others willingly and wholeheartedly, with sincerity. In doing so, not only will the individual be blessed by your actions, but you will too.

Who can you serve today, and how can you serve them?

Great Leaders Take Responsibility for Their Actions

Have you ever played the blame game before? More times than not, I blame others for my mistakes. If we are honest, at some point in our life we don't always own up to our own shortcomings. Has there ever been an incident where you blamed other people for your actions and behavior? Think about that for a moment.

I grew up with three stepbrothers and cousins about the same age as me, and we didn't always get along. We usually fought and bickered a couple of times during the day, which tended to drive our parents crazy. Like me, if you have siblings or cousins and something went wrong when you were together, I'm sure it was easy to point fingers and say, "They did it." You put the blame on them rather than yourself. Why is that? At the time of the incident, I'm sure you didn't want to get any consequences that went along with it. That is totally understandable. However, while it is easier to blame others for your own mistakes, that could only make the situation worse. Taking responsibility for your own actions and behaviors, though, will have a lasting impact on you and your future endeavors.

The Lord detests lying lips, but He delights in those who tell the truth.
—*Proverbs 12:22 (NLT)*

I love to work with children around age four or five. Whenever a couple of them are in a room together, something usually goes wrong that you didn't plan for. Someone hits or kicks another, toys are taken, and tears can be shed because a child has gotten hurt. Many things can happen. One thing I have come to realize with kids and people in general is that no one likes to get in trouble. When a child does, most of the time their natural tendency is to lie and blame the incident on another child. As a teacher, there is no way that I can have my eye on every child every minute of the day. I'm human, so I don't always catch everything that happens. Well, on this Friday afternoon, something did happen. One of the boys, Teddy, took a toy from Justin. Now, Teddy and Justin didn't know I was watching the whole encounter when it took place. So when the incident occurred, and tears and hollering were starting to arise, I asked both children to come and tell me what had happened. Both children began to speak and explain the situation, but Teddy began to lie. He knew he was in trouble and didn't want to accept the consequences. Being that Teddy took the toy from Justin, I made him apologize and give it back. Since he hadn't told me the truth to begin with, I made him sit alone and think about the decision that he had made before he went back to playing.

When we don't take responsibility for our actions and cover them up with a lie, the person or people involved seem to have a harder punishment than the people who were honest about the situation in the first place. Although Teddy apologized and gave the toy back to Justin, there was still a consequence because of his actions. Not just with the toy, but because he hadn't told me the truth to start with. He wanted another child to take the blame for the actions he chose, which caused more punishment in the long run.

It can happen not only with children but with adults as well. Adults can blame their behavior and actions on others whom they are around. That doesn't fix the problem but only makes it worst. While blaming others can be the easy way out, it never truly solves the issue. You are less likely to leave the situation with a guilty conscience when you take ownership and responsibility for your actions. Telling the truth also allows you to be well respected by your peers. Although it isn't necessarily the easiest thing to do, great leaders don't blame their mistakes on others. They acknowledge their own faults and come forward with the truth from the very beginning.

Do you have anything to come clean about in your own life? If yes, explain.

Why do you think you haven't told the truth before now?

Great Leaders Confront Conflict

Dealing with conflict is something that no one wants to handle. If it is not confronted, the situation usually ends with a destroyed relationship and begrudging feelings. More times than not, we are going to come across someone that we don't necessarily get along with. You might have different personalities, making you two clash. It is hard to work with them if you have to. Whether it is a person that you work with, someone in your school, or a member in your family, we need to be showing kindness to one another even if we don't see eye to eye on certain things. Although it can be challenging, we are called to live in unity with one another.

Blessed are the peacemakers: for they shall be called the children of God.
—Matthew 5:9 (KJV)

A couple of years ago, I was chosen to stay a year in North Carolina on an internship working at Snowbird. The girls and guys were put into groups doing certain jobs around campus for that year. The guys mainly worked in maintenance, while the girls maintained cleaning and scheduling around camp. Now, we (the interns) all knew one another from prior summers, but we were all scattered doing different things. There were nine girls who worked together closely around camp and we quickly discovered that our personalities didn't always mesh very well.

A few weeks went by, and the leader of the group, Carly, saw that we were all not working together as a team. We were not being unified like we should, which made for a very awkward and agonizing year ahead if we didn't confront the problems from the start. She knew that all of us had different personalities, and it wasn't easy working with each other because of it.

Hopefully, great leaders should want to invest in the lives of others, so Carly was the mentor to us all, knowing that whatever we said to her, she would keep it confidential. Whenever one of the girls had an issue with another, she would always listen and give counsel as needed. Since so many of us girls were talking about the problems we faced with coworkers, she knew enough was enough and wanted to nip in it the bud before the problems got worse.

One night, while we were off work, Carly called all of us girls together to discuss our issues with one another. No one wanted to come out and say what we didn't like about another person. Therefore, she made us go around and share what we could be doing better as a group. Although it was hard, it was an eye-opener. As a leader, it is important to take all sides into consideration. Carly wanted to help resolve the issues at hand, not add to them or let them fester. She approached us girls with humility, not judgment, wanting to mend the broken relationships before they escalated into something more.

Not only does confrontation affect you, but it affects the people around you as well. Since the girls that I worked with didn't get along too well, that made the job less enjoyable and affected the staff as a whole. This friction caused issues among our daily jobs and relationships with other people. Without realizing it, I would be discussing an issue with a fellow coworker that I didn't need to be involved in the first place. Soon, that began to cause rivalry among the team. Carly, being the great leader that she was, wanted to help from the beginning. She was not a bother or a hindrance but a huge help throughout the intern year. Although us girls managed to get along as the year progressed, we eventually realized that we weren't only damaging ourselves but others as well. With that being said, all of us decided to mend the strained relationships. Although it was hard to admit, we all needed to have a change of heart. Each one of us knew that we needed to work on certain things internally in order to get along for the sake of the group and the summer staff that would be approaching in just a few short weeks.

How do you approach conflict?

Is it hard for you to confront conflict? If yes, why do you think that is?

What are some steps you can take to resolve conflict once it starts rather than letting it linger?

Great Leaders Lead by Example

Remember your leaders who taught you the word of God. Think of all the good that has come from their lives, and follow the example of their faith.
—*Hebrews 13:7 (NLT)*

Back in the olden days, the boss or leader of that time would usually sit on a chair called a throne. This throne would be made of gold or bronze to symbolize the importance of the person who sat upon it. If the boss wanted to go somewhere, their slaves and servants carried them wherever they wished to go. All they had to do was dictate their orders, and the slaves followed, obeying their command...easy, right? Sometimes I wish my life were like that. However, I'm sure that the people helping carry the throne weren't having much fun. Not only was the throne heavy, but the slaves and servants were constantly hearing their boss talk down to them as they worked.

Having someone bark orders at you isn't ideal either. When someone does demean you, it makes you less effective and reduces your self-confidence.

Leaders don't just demand orders and tell others what to do. In my opinion, that would be considered a boss. Great leaders lead by example. They lead by their actions and their attitudes, showing how to do the task well no matter what it involves. Recently, I saw a video of three men who were pulling one man on a sled. The man who was sitting was whipping his servants while also shouting to move at a faster pace. Needless to say, because of the man's actions, it was very difficult for the three men to keep pulling him to his destination. Right below this video, I quickly discovered another. The video below was similar yet gave off a different meaning. Instead of the leader sitting on the sled, he was pulling it along with his slaves. The leader was the person in the front of the pack, motivating and helping his people accomplish the goal. That is what a great leader should strive to do.

When a person leads by example, they are modeling what to do along with how to act when doing a task. Someone who is a leader doesn't just sit back, dictate orders, and watch it happen. They are at the forefront, encouraging others to keep going and push forward. Not only does this grow your self-confidence, but it also enables you to do a better job when you see that your leader isn't slacking. You can't expect other people to do their best if you aren't putting in your best effort yourself. When your leader is putting their all into a task, you should too. Great leaders are easy to follow, knowing that they will be alongside you to accomplish and endure the task at hand no matter what arises. They are in it with you, struggle and all.

No matter your age, being a leader is something you choose. Whether you are a seventh grader trying to fit in, a first-year college student, or a struggling parent, it is up to you whether or not to embrace great leadership qualities. Remember, someone is always going to be looking up to you, and you are always going to be looking up to someone else, whether you know it or not. Maybe you are the person on the throne only watching others work. Don't just sit on the sidelines and give direction where it is needed. I encourage you to get your hands dirty. Yes, it may involve effort that you may not necessarily want to put forth. Give it your best shot from the very beginning. Maybe you are a follower (like I was) who is afraid to branch out and go their own way. Be the person God has created you to be, a confident individual who stands out from the crowd. Take it from me: if you want to be a great leader, you need to model it with your actions as well as your behavior. In turn, hopefully others will follow your example and build up others that please the Lord.

Do you consider yourself to be a boss or a leader?

What qualities do you possess that give off that vibe?

Who Are You Going to Follow?

Social Media

In today's society, it is no secret that most people have a social media account. I remember when I got my first one. For the record, it wasn't Myspace. (Remember when that was popular?) I thought I was one of the cool kids. Little did I know that social media can have a huge effect on you. Now, not all social media is bad. Although I wholeheartedly think it is how the user chooses to view it that can lead to bondage. Twitter, Facebook, Instagram, or TikTok can all be viewed from a phone or computer within just a few seconds. With just a few taps of your fingers, it can lead to hours scrolling up and down to see the hottest gossip or latest video trend. It is so mind-boggling how far our generation has come with technology.

Just for fun, I googled the average hours a person is on social media in one day. The results were shocking, to say the least. According to Statista, the average person spends 147 minutes on social media every day. Facebook users spend roughly 38 minutes per day. Twitter fans spend up to 35 minutes, TikTok is 46 minutes, and the highest is Instagram, capping out at 53 minutes a day. Wow! To be honest, when I read those stats, I wasn't surprised. Say we have all four of those accounts; we would spend up to four hours numbing ourselves on social media. Every. Single. Day. I get that everyone is different, and it varies some, but my point is still the same. We live in a world that has technology at our fingertips. Don't get me wrong; social media can be a great asset to us. But it can also pull us into a world that isn't reality.

If I scrolled on your feed right now, what would I see? Would I see words of encouragement or negativity? Would I see videos of worldly pleasures? Do you change the screen when someone enters the room? Are you looking at something that you think you are keeping private? Most importantly, what would God see? That is the bigger question. Well, God sees, and God knows. The enemy is crafty and makes things look enticing that only satisfy you in the moment and for the moment. That is his goal. There is a passage in scripture that talks about giving the enemy a foothold (Ephesians 4:27). This means that you shouldn't let the enemy have even an ounce of influence over your life and your decisions. How do you do it? You meet the enemy at the door and leave him there. Don't invite him into your thoughts. Don't let him enter and allow him to disrupt your mind, creating lies and schemes to ruin your life. It all starts with your mind. If you think it, soon you will begin to believe it and act upon it. Let me explain.

Celebrities, I think, can be the brunt of all social media platforms. In today's day and age, they don't have to do much to get the media's attention. News about their every move seems to be plastered in the next magazine or news article that comes into the stores. Not only articles but also pictures that might give people the wrong impression about them. Now, I'm sure that they get tired of people trying to capture their every move. I mean, wouldn't you? It is no secret that the paparazzi follow them constantly, trying to capture the facts and get the real story behind the celebrity. But do they know who and what they are really capturing? Reality is, the latest gossip and photograph about their lives will fade in the next twenty-four hours; then something or someone else will come into the limelight. I've known so many people that do things celebrities do simply because they are popular. People get caught up in things all because celebrities are doing them. That simply isn't right. Like the latest fashion trend, their popularity is fleeting too. You don't have to be popular for people to notice you. Take initiative. Be the change that the world needs. If you want to see more positive posts, start with you. If you want to see more pleasing trends, start with you. You can make a difference for the better. So be bold, be brave, and be wise on social media.

In what ways has technology affected your life?

How can you be wise and make good judgment on social media?

Do you post for your own praise or for God's praise?

Let me give you a visual aid. I am not a big social media person, but I do get on every now and again. I mainly use it to keep in contact with friends and family that live in other states. Usually when I get on, I tend to scroll to see if anything new is happening. I often see pictures of my friends smiling and laughing, a lot of times with their spouses and kids. Some are visiting different places around the world that usually involve a coffee cup in hand. Then I start playing the comparison game, and my head begins to fill up with lies and imperfections about myself. My brain starts thinking, *They look so happy. It must be nice to travel to that place. I wonder if that is where so-and-so met. I need to go to different places so I can hopefully meet my future spouse. I wish I had a job that would allow me to travel. I'm sure no new job would hire me because of my age and past. If I don't have a new job, I can't travel and hopefully find my person. Not only that, but I'm not pretty like she is. In high school, she was in beauty pageants and won most of the time. She also has a great sense of humor and personality to match. Being that I can't travel, I am average, and I'm not that funny, I won't ever get married, have kids, or be as happy as my friend in this picture.*

Now, that was a very dramatic example, but I wanted to give you a sense of the lies that the enemy can throw your way. He wants you to see all the fun and happiness on the outside yet wants to conceal the troubles behind the picture. It's one thing to show the joyful times but another to show how you're really feeling in the moment, the side the camera doesn't portray. Therefore, you start comparing yourself to the person in the picture rather than the person behind the picture. You are only going to see what you are willing to see. Don't let that thought creep into your mind; take it captive.

Don't let it escape more into your thoughts, wanting to destroy your happiness and self-esteem. Set your mind on things that are from above. Think about all the blessings that God has given you rather than comparing yourself to someone you are not. Rather than thinking those lies, I could speak blessings and say, *That is so great that they took this trip. It is well deserved. God surely blessed them with a job that allows them to travel to different places. It also is a wonderful blessing that they get to travel with family. It gives them time to be together, which makes them happy. Also, I may not be as pretty as she is, but I've got friends and family that support and love me. They seem to think I'm funny and have a great personality regardless of what I think about myself. God made me a masterpiece, so I'll live it up to the fullest, knowing that I am made simply unique.*

Instead of saying "Why me?" say "Why not me?" I admit it can be easy playing the comparison game, but that doesn't make it right. People are all going through their own struggles. Many show the world only the fun times and not the hardships life can have to offer. Therefore, if we are all going through seasons of struggle, why compare? God gave you everything you need to be successful in this life. You are the only you there is. Be grateful and mindful of that. Take ownership of it. You are living the life that God created you to live, not anyone else.

When you see pictures of people on social media, do you compare yourself to them?

Rather than thinking negatively, what can you do differently to speak positivity about yourself?

The Ultimate Leader

In my opinion, Jesus is the ultimate example to follow. He never sinned and continued to please the Lord in whatever He chose to do. Although He led a life that was perfect, by no means was it easy. Jesus went through all of the struggles we will ever endure, yet He did not sin. He did not give in to those temptations of sinful actions but was made more like Christ because of His endurance during those trying times. I choose to follow Jesus, the epitome of perfection.

Like I mentioned before, you are always going to be following someone in your life, whether that person is physically here on Earth or not. What do I mean by this? As a Christian, I wholeheartedly believe that there is both a Savior and an enemy in the world today, with Jesus being the Savior of the world (1 John 4:14) and Satan being the ruler of the world (Ephesians 2:2, Revelation 12:9). People who don't surrender their life to Jesus are called unbelievers, only submitting to sin (worldly things) and obeying their own fleshly desires. Once you become a believer, however, you are called to submit your life to Jesus and follow on the path that He has for you. No longer are you following the world's standards, but God's standards.

Satan wants you to live a life that is full of sin. Although the sin may seem pleasing momentarily it will only lead to devastation and torment in the long run. Satan wants you to suffer, experience pain and hardship, and go against God by any means necessary. He doesn't want you to live a Godly lifestyle, but a corrupt one. God, though, is the complete opposite. Those who believe in Him will experience true joy, confidence, and peace. God loves you so much that He has already forgiven you for your sins by dying on a cross. He wants to make you whole and a new creation, ultimately changing your heart for the better. If you consider yourself to be a good person, that simply isn't enough. Without Christ, something will always be missing from your life. Being a follower of the Lord means that you are surrendering your life over to Him, and only Him. As the scripture says, you can't serve two masters (Matthew 6:24). You make the decision as to whom you serve and put your trust in. You either serve God or Satan (fleshly desires). Remember, though, whom you serve will lead to eternal consequences, either Heaven or Hell (Galatians 6:7–8).

You may be thinking that you want to become a believer. That's the best decision you will ever make, and I pray that you do, but you may not know how. So, how do you surrender your life over to Jesus? It is quite simple. There is no right or wrong way to do it. If you are feeling God leading you in that direction, I urge you to repeat these words with sincerity and pray to Him. "Jesus, I know I am a sinner. I know I have followed my own path. I know that I have messed up and have done things that I am not proud of. God, I ask You to come into my heart and save me from my sins. I'm sorry for the things that I have done. I ask You to forgive me. Take these things from me. Lord, I surrender my life over to you. Lead me in your way and teach me how to become a better person. Help me to put my faith and trust in you. Thank you for dying on the cross and saving me. In Jesus's name, amen."

Chapter 4
Accountability

Confess your sins to one another and pray for one another, that you may be healed. The prayer of a righteous person has great power as it is working.

—*James 5:16 (ESV)*

If you have been around Christians at some point, they might talk about their accountability partner. This person is usually someone that you can go to for advice and share your struggles and problems to without judgment, someone who wants you to become a better person. If you or a friend has an accountability partner, that simply means that they are going to remind you of your goal and push you closer to it, i.e., as believers, living like Christ. Life can be chaotic, busy, and stressful at times. Therefore, accountability partners help set goals for you and make sure they are followed through. They want to see you succeed. In the end, though, it is ultimately your responsibility to make your goals a reality.

Maybe this accountability partner is something you have never heard of before. You may not want to share your struggles and joys with someone else, and that's fine; however, at some point, we all need to vent once in a while. I know that it helps me feel better when I talk things out with someone. Therefore, I desperately advise you to find one person, preferably the same gender, that you can share your heart with, knowing that they will listen and give wise feedback when needed.

Be Trustworthy

Anyone can be an accountability partner for someone. I encourage you to be mindful of whom you share personal information with. Can that person be trusted with the information you are giving them? Having someone that you can trust is vital. Whether that person is a member of your family, a teacher, or a coworker, you have to be sure that whatever you say to them is confidential. If the person gossiped to you about others, most likely they are gossiping to others about you. You don't want to share all of your problems to them and they go and blab about it to someone else. People go to people whom they trust. Take that into consideration when looking for an accountability partner. Is this person someone with integrity? Can I trust them with my problems?

When someone asks you to be their accountability partner, you need to keep your mouth shut also. It should be considered an honor, and you don't want to take the position lightly. The person trusts you with their issues. So don't gossip to others or ask for other people's opinion on the situation. That is why I advise others to seek accountability from people older and wiser than themselves. It is okay to talk to your friends about stuff. When it comes to personal advice, however, you are going through the same stage of life as your friends, especially if you are in middle or high school. With that being said, your friends don't always know how to help your situation because most of the time, they haven't gone through it yet.

This is why I encourage you to seek counsel from people who have already gone through those struggles themselves.

What qualities do you look for in an accountability partner?

Does your accountability partner push you to become a better person? If so, how?

Tough Love—Be Blunt, Not Harsh

Instead, we will speak the truth in love, growing in every way more and more like Christ, who is the head of his body, the church.
—Ephesians 4:15 (NLT)

Having an accountability partner doesn't always mean that things will go smoothly for you. Again, it is important that you are helping to point them in the right direction. On occasion that might mean hearing things that you don't necessarily want to hear. Having certain people speak into your life, though, will not only help you grow your relationship with God, but they can catch the blind spots that you might be missing.

While I was at camp, I was chosen to mentor three other staff members throughout the summer. Within the first couple of weeks, we got to know each other and became very close. Each of us girls got to meet regularly to discuss what was happening in our lives and shared what we could do to better ourselves as Christians. As the weeks went by, it became evident that one of the girls was starting to have feelings for a guy who worked on staff. When I first approached her about the situation, she quickly became defensive and denied it. She didn't want to be caught or own up to her feelings. At first, I let it slide. I wanted to see if it was truly becoming a distraction for her. Days went on, and I started to notice that she was starting to get very clingy toward him, as well as spending more and more time with him rather than doing her job. Needless to say, she was losing focus on why she came to camp in the first place: to help students and herself grow in their walk with the Lord.

Since I was her mentor, once again I approached her about the situation. I knew it had to be addressed before it got out of hand. One afternoon, I asked her about the guy and if any feelings were there. This time she owned up to liking him but didn't see the problem that was occurring within the situation. She was only focused on herself and her feelings for him, not seeing the bigger picture and how this distraction affected others too. Before I went any further into the conversation, I asked her, "You know I love you and want the best for you right?" I wanted her to know that I was coming from a place of love, wanting her to not be distracted in ministry. She responded with "Yes." Since she knew that I wasn't trying to shame or demean her, I began to explain my thought process toward her behavior. Basically, how she was being distracted by her feelings and neglecting her own responsibilities because she was only focused on a guy. I didn't sugarcoat anything. I told it to her like it was, saying what she needed to hear and not what she wanted to hear. Although it was hard to swallow by my explanation, she could tell that it was becoming a problem that had to be fixed.

When you approach a situation, it can go one of two ways. Either the person can get defensive, or they hear you out and take what you say into consideration. If you are the one being mentored, hear what your mentor has to say. Initially, your accountability partner might ask questions and call out things in your life that may be a hindrance toward your goal. They don't need to beat around the bush when speaking into your life. They notice things that might be an issue and call it out willingly. Yet they approach the situation with love and not judgment or aggression. If you consider them to be an accountability partner, you should trust them enough to speak into your life and want the best for it, regardless of how you might feel. They are there to help you succeed and be there for you as a support system.

On the other hand, if you ever mentor someone and they suddenly get mad and want to end the friendship, begin to pray for them. Ask the Lord to help them see what He needs them to see. You can be a friend, showing that you care, but a little tough love might be in order. Sometimes that may ruin a friendship. I've seen it happen, especially if you share the Gospel with someone that doesn't want to hear it. I think it is important to say that the Gospel is offensive. Some people don't want anything to do with it because it brings out their own mistakes and shortcomings. Although that's what it was made to do, so Jesus can wipe our slate clean, others don't see it that way. While some people may understand and internalize this, some don't want to. Understand that you are not responsible for how they react to the conversation. What you are responsible for is being there for them as a friend and as a mentor. You can only control you. The way they respond is up to the individual.

Do you have an accountability partner? If so, who?

What attributes do they possess that make them a good one?

Would you consider being an accountability partner to someone?

No Judgment Here

Cast your burden onto the Lord, and He will sustain you. He will never permit the righteous to be moved.

—Psalm 55:22 (ESV)

When you are an accountability partner for someone or vice versa, it is crucial that no judgment occurs. Now, I understand that we are all human and make mistakes. However, once the person notices that you are judging them, it can only go downhill from there. Many people have opened up to me and shared personal things that I didn't think they would ever go through. Although it was hard to keep my composure, I let them speak and then gently yet boldly gave my advice. I have a friend who considers me her person. Whenever she is struggling or has a problem, she comes to me knowing that I won't judge or shame her for it while also giving her wise counsel.

Remember Carly from the previous chapter? Carly listened to all the intern girls' problems without judging or shaming us. During the group meeting, she was trusted to keep what we said confidential as she approached us all with gentleness yet was firm and told each of us what we needed to hear. If you are asked to be someone's accountability partner, don't judge their life choices based on your own experiences. Be gracious and listen with sincerity.

Jesus spoke about being judgmental in the book of John. While Jesus was teaching in the Temple, a huge crowd gathered around to hear Him. As He was speaking, the Philistines brought a woman in and placed her in front of Jesus and the crowd. This woman was caught in the act of adultery.

By this time, the whole crowd knew her sin that she had committed. The Philistines didn't want to keep her sin quiet but chose to announce it in front of everyone. They were judging the woman's sin. Not only was she an adulterer, but she was caught in the act. Could you imagine the embarrassment and shame she must have felt? No longer was her sin kept secret, but the Philistines quickly exposed it without any consideration for the woman. The Philistines then began to tell Jesus about the woman's sin and that she should be stoned. "What do you say?" they asked Jesus. Instead of responding negatively, Jesus bent down and wrote these powerful words in the sand: "Let the one who has never sinned throw the first stone" (John 8:7, NLT).

Reading this, one by one the crowd backed away until only Jesus and the woman were left standing in the middle of the crowd.

Just like the adulterous woman, everyone will make mistakes. There is not one person on this earth who is or will ever be perfect. A lot of times, I don't want to own up to my own shortcomings. I make a lot of mistakes on a daily basis, too many to count. It sometimes can be challenging to voice our problems or mistakes to others when they do happen. It can be scary because you don't want to feel like you are being judged by others in the process. Why not go to someone who will never judge or shame you for what you have done? The Lord has already forgiven you for every mistake you have made and will make in the future, big or small. When you pray and ask the Lord to forgive it, He does wholeheartedly. The Bible says that God is the ultimate judge. No one is better than anyone else, and every sin is the same in God's eyes. With that being said, who are we to judge others when we make mistakes ourselves?

Why do you think it can be hard to share your struggles with someone?

Do you feel like people are judging you for your mistakes? Why or why not?

Do you tend to judge others for their mistakes?

We Are All Accountable

Have you ever been to a cemetery before? I have been to my share of funerals at cemeteries and actually live relatively close to one now. Sometimes my mom and I walk down to it to get some exercise. Once we get into the cemetery, we will walk around the loop and see if there are any new grave sites. Now, if someone has passed away, what do you think is the most important thing on a headstone? The name of the person? The dates that they lived? Maybe it's the picture on the tombstone? Well, these are all wrong. Not that these aren't important, but the most crucial thing on that tombstone is the dash that connects the person's birthday to their death date.

You may be asking, why is that so significant? The dash resembles how the person has lived. You might forget the name of the person, their birthday, or even the day that they passed, but you never forget their life and how it impacted you.

Everyone will be held accountable for their life choices. No one is exempt. The Bible speaks about something called the end times. As a Christian, I believe that every person is going to stand before the Lord once they die and give an account for themselves. If you consider yourself to believe in God, you are called to tell others about Him, living a lifestyle that reflects the Lord and shines His light on others.

Here comes my next question: How will people remember you? Are you helpful and a blessing to those around you? Some may say that you have a kind and gentle soul, always wanting to be there for others. These are all great qualities to have. However, what ultimately matters is your love for the Lord. Will people say that you strived to be a godly example to others? Will they say that your life pointed others to Christ? What have you done with His name? In the Bible, it talks about getting to Heaven and seeing the pearly gates open wide, welcoming people in. If you are not a believer and have not accepted Christ into your heart, unfortunately you are not welcome. In Matthew 25:23, Jesus is speaking to those who have passed. As a believer, it is my goal to hear the words "Well done my good and faithful servant" from the Lord when I leave this earth. Others, though, may not believe. If that is the case, Jesus will say, "Depart from me. I never knew you." What are you doing for the Lord?

Let me ask you this: If you had the cure for cancer, would you tell people about it? Hopefully you would because it will help millions of people battling this disease so that they might live. If you feel that others need to hear it, why not share about this news? When it comes to nonbelievers, the Gospel is what they truly need to hear. Once you believe in God, you have the antidote for spiritual death and for eternal life (Christ) in your heart. Are you sharing and telling others about Him? Many people say they have Christ in their life, but they don't act upon it or share His love with others, hindering them from eternal life. It's a sad reality but so very true.

How are you making the most out of your life right now?

What are you doing now that will have a lasting impact on others?

Chapter 5
Obedience Isn't Optional

Seek first the Kingdom of God above all else, and live righteously, and He will give you everything you need.

– Matthew 6:33 (NLT)

I'm sure by now, you already know that I love movies and reference them quite a lot. Usually many of the movies that I watch have some type of message intertwined throughout the story. These stories tend to make me wonder about my own life within certain aspects. The movie *Ella Enchanted* is no exception. Let me explain.

At the beginning of this movie, a baby named Ella is born. A couple of days after her birth, Ella's fairy godmother, Lucinda, comes into her family's home, wanting to grant the new child a gift. All of this may sound great, but Lucinda was credited with giving the gifts that no one wanted. When the fairy entered the cottage, she thought and thought of the perfect gift to give the babe while holding her in her arms. Now, as most babies do, Ella began to cry when her godmother held her. Lucinda couldn't seem to calm Ella down, so what gift did she bestow upon the child? The gift of obedience.

You might be thinking, *This is great! Obedience would make a wonderful gift.* However, in the movie, you begin to see that it isn't as wonderful as Lucinda made it out to be. Now, we don't have a magical fairy to make us become obedient, like in the movie. We must simply choose to become obedient ourselves. I understand this is a great feat that no one can master in a day, a week, or probably even a lifetime. You might be thinking that you don't want to obey anyone; you just want to do your own thing as you walk through life. As we look into this chapter, I encourage and challenge you to think about the word obedience and what that means to you. As we dig deeper, I advise you to reflect on your own obedience. What does that look like in your own life?

First, in order to become obedient, we must know what it means. In the dictionary, the word obedience means compliance with an order, request, or law, or submission to another's authority. Being obedient is something that is challenging for me to do. It isn't always the easiest thing, nor is it the most enjoyable at times. It can lead you to do things that are difficult or scary while also leading you on a path to success. What do I mean by this? Read and find out.

Whom Should You Obey?

I think it is vital to know whom we should obey so we can get more insight on how we should obey. We should all be obedient in our lives. Although it can be strenuous, the end goal is worth it. A word of caution, though, be careful as to whom you obey, even if that is yourself. By taking one small step in God's obedience, though, you will see the fruitfulness and faithfulness that flows from it.

Parents

For all authority comes from God, and those positions of authority have been placed there by God. So anyone who rebels against authority is rebelling against what God has instituted.

—Romans 13:1–2 (NLT)

Seeing parents on the list first probably isn't your first choice. Your parents might set all of these strict rules you have to follow. Some of you might have parents that seem to only care about their job or significant other rather than investing in you. Whatever the case may be, scripture is not just telling us but commanding us to obey them.

As stated in scripture in Exodus 20:12, it says to honor your father and mother. Easier said than done, am I right? This task can be hard to do, especially if your parents are not believers. "Do your homework. Take the trash out. Do your chores. Don't stay out past curfew." Sound familiar? Now, you have one of two options. Option one: you roll your eyes, mumble under your breath, sigh heavily to make sure your parents notice, and then do what they have asked while complaining and grumbling the whole time. Option two: you don't do what your parents have asked, and in turn, you get the consequences for your actions. So, if obeying your parents is tough and not necessarily ideal, why should we do it?

When your parents ask you to do something, what is your first tendency... option one or option two?

Since neither of the options were necessarily the best, what is something that you can do to prevent that tendency from happening?

God's Word teaches us the importance of obedience, especially obeying your parents. God thought it is so important He needed to put it in the Bible four different times. You can read about it in Colossians 3:20, Ephesians 6:1, Exodus 20:21, and Ephesians 6:23. Not only that, but it is the only commandment with a promise. Ephesians 6:1-3 states: "Children, obey your parents in the Lord, for this is right. Honor your father and mother—which is the first commandant with a promise—so that it may go well with you and that you enjoy a long life on the earth" (NIV).

So, what's the promise? Is it saying that because you obey your parents you will be guaranteed a long life with no problems? Absolutely not. I am here to tell you that since you are on this earth, you will have hardships and difficulties. That is for certain. Also, no one knows when they will die, so it can't be promising that you will live a full life until you are old and gray. Scripture is enforcing that God gave you to your parents for a reason. He entrusted them to take care of you and provide for you while on the earth. Since God gave them authority over your life, you are accountable for your behavior and actions. Does that mean you have to agree with everything they ask or say? No. However, how you act while doing it indicates that you love and respect your parents enough to do what they have asked even though you might not understand it in the moment.

Believe it or not, your parents were once teenagers going through the same things you experience, more or less. Because of this, your parents know what is best for you even though you may not understand it at the time. Maybe your parents aren't believers, and you have a hard time obeying them because they go against God's Word. This can be challenging. I advise you to pray and seek a mentor and godly adult that you trust to help you navigate this obstacle. Praying for your parents is the best thing you can do for them.

Now, I want to be very careful on how I approach this. If your parents are telling you to do things that endanger you or could get you into trouble, then don't stand for it. Everyone has their issues and mess-ups. Maybe they are into things like drugs or alcohol. I know a few of my students whose moms or dads are in jail for a significant amount of time. Some of you might have a parent that is abusive (emotionally and/or physically) toward you. You don't have to obey someone if they want you to do wrongful things. You know what is truly right in your heart and mind. Remember, you have a choice in the matter too. So seek a mentor, counselor, or adult, anyone you trust to help you and get you out of that situation. Informing someone about it does not make you weak or shameful but courageous and brave.

If your parent(s) are like this, what is something you can do to stand up for yourself and seek help if needed?

One last thing: my youth pastor reminds us daily that obeying your parents can give others a glimpse of how you obey the Lord. Are you motivated and willing to obey your parents at whatever task they give? How about the Lord? Take that into consideration. That is why seeking the Lord is so important. Although your parents might make mistakes and disappoint you, I encourage you to submit to God's authority, for He will never steer you wrong. Remember, God gave your parents authority over you for a reason. Even though you may not agree a lot of the time, your job is to submit to their authority and obey them as the Lord intended.

What are some ways you can honor your parents while having the right attitude at the same time?

Earthly Masters

Slaves, obey your earthly masters in everything you do. Try to please them all the time, not just when they are watching you. Serve them sincerely because of your reverent fear of the Lord.

—Colossians 3:22 (NLT)

Many people can fall into this category. Look back at chapter three, "Following the Leader." The same individuals whom you consider to be leaders in your life can also be earthly masters in your life. My mind goes right to a boss or a teacher. Yet these are only two of the many earthly masters in your life. This might be a sensitive topic for some, but the message is still the same. It states two times in scripture to obey your earthly masters (Ephesians 6:5–9 and Colossians 3:22). The Lord is pretty clear as to who you obey. However, like I mentioned earlier, if they tell you to do something that isn't biblical or is against the law, you have to use your own judgment to overcome that obstacle with maturity and wisdom.

Scripture states that we are to respect our earthly masters' authority while also working wholeheartedly and serving sincerely. Whether that person is a believer of not, many times, if someone tells me to do a task that I don't want to do, my first tendency is to grumble and complain. That does me no good. Especially in the workplace, sometimes I don't want to do the task assigned. I want to do enough just to scrape by, not wanting to go the extra mile and put forth additional effort. Although that is sometimes my tendency, I should want to have a Christ-like attitude when obeying my earthly masters. God said we are to work as though we are working for the Lord rather than for people. In the verse stated above, it says that we are to serve them because we serve the Lord. Not because we enjoy the task. Not because we will get paid. Not because our parents/boss told us we have to, but because of our willingness to follow God's obedience. You see, because of our willingness to obey even when we don't want to, we not only show others a good work ethic but also hopefully point them to the serving heart of God. He sees the effort being presented. He sees your heart behind your work ethic. Instead of letting your attitude get the best of you, learn to cope. Listen to Christian music or an inspirational podcast while you work. Keep reminding yourself of verses from scripture about grumbling and complaining. Keep your mindset focused on the Lord and not the people involved.

Do you tend to give half effort or go the extra mile for your earthly masters? Why?

How do you think the Lord feels about your attitude and actions while doing the task assigned?

Just like obeying your parents, God has placed authority over your life for a reason. You are always going to have to submit to someone's authority in your life as long as you live. How you treat your bosses, teachers, coaches, etc., will stem from how you treat and respect God's authority over your life.

God or Flesh

In the movie, Lucinda put a spell on Ella to instantly make her become obedient. Let me be blunt. God isn't like that. He doesn't put a spell on us, turning us into robots, making us do His every will the way He wants it done. If God did that, there would be no reason to trust Him. Instead, He gave us the ability to make our own decisions and submit to our own authority, creating free will.

Why do you think it is important that God gives us the option to choose or reject Him?

When I wrote the word flesh in the heading, I was indicating that we have a choice to make. We can either follow the Lord and what He has for us, or we can follow our own path in our flesh. You can give in to it and suffer the consequences, or you can reject that sin and turn the other cheek. If God hadn't allowed free choice, we would all be slaves to Him. Everyone on the earth would love Him without any options. Matthew 16:24 states that you cannot serve two masters. So who are you going to serve, God or the enemy?

Let's say a spell was cast on someone you like. This spell made the person fall madly in love with you. Would you be truly happy that the person loved you because he/she was under a spell? I know I wouldn't. The same thing happens with God. By giving the world free choice, we are choosing whether to love God or not. We have a choice to make, according to Joshua 24:15. We can either love God with all our being or reject Him as Lord and Savior of our lives.

There is not a single person in the world that is perfect. I think I have established that. Because of this, the enemy likes to put things in our path to make us choose our way instead of God's way. Every time you lie, cheat, steal, and complain, those are all tendencies of your flesh. Being tempted does not make you sinful; it makes you human. Acting upon the temptation, however, can lead you further away from the Lord while delving into sin. The Lord doesn't make us sin; the enemy doesn't even make you sin. You yourself are guilty. Satan only planted the idea in your mind, but you acted upon it, making it your own. The enemy's job is to steel your joy, kill your faith, and destroy your testimony (John 10:10). He wants to whisper things in your ear that make you doubt the Lord and His plan for you. Don't give into those fleshly desires or temptations that might occur. Seek God through it all and surrender your life to Him.

Submitting to God's authority is the most humbling and faith-seeking thing you can do as a believer. It allows you to grow yourself like never before. Remember when I was applying to work at camp? I was so nervous yet excited when I finally let God take over and submitted to His authority. In order to obey the Lord, you have to hear when He is speaking to you. That, in turn, comes with knowing who He is and having a relationship with Him. I had to listen to Him; that all starts with reading and meditating on scripture, something I have mentioned already. Once you know the Lord, that doesn't mean obeying Him will become instant. It can be a challenge, like anything, to go against the world and seek the Lord in scripture. Nevertheless, we should live by God's standards and not the world's. God's standards are evident in Exodus 20:1–17 and Galatians 5:22–23:

> You shall have no other Gods before me. (Make God the only God of your life.)
>
> You shall not make any idols. (My God is a jealous God.)
>
> You shall not take the name of the Lord in vain. (Don't misuse God's name.)
>
> Remember the Sabbath day and keep it holy. (Sunday is a day to honor the Lord by going to church and truly resting and worshipping Him.)
>
> Honor your father and mother. (Obey and respect them.)
>
> You shall not murder. (Do not kill or hurt others.)
>
> You shall not commit adultery. (Don't cheat.)
>
> You shall not steal.
>
> You shall not bear false witness against your neighbor. (Don't lie.)
>
> You shall not covet. (Don't be jealous.)

The fruit of the Spirit is love, joy, peace, patience, kindness, goodness, faithfulness, gentleness, and self-control.

—Galatians 5:22–23 (ESV)

This comes with a lot of prayer and discipline. No one will be a master at this overnight. It is a daily submission to Christ. Once you do it and begin to seek Him out for yourself, the more evident He will be in your life. If you are not obedient in the small things God has for you, you won't be obedient in the big things either. It all starts with one small step. Let go and let God take control.

What benefits do God's standards provide that the world's standards don't?

I hope to become a mom one day if the Lord sees fit. Ever since I was young, I always loved babies, so I hope to have some of my own someday. Now, a baby doesn't just get up and start running when it is a newborn. There is a process. It gradually sits up on its own and then starts to crawl, which eventually leads to walking. Once mobile, the baby has to take small steps in order to get from place to place. As their body gets bigger, they can make grander strides. It has the same effect with us as believers. God wants us to take small steps of obedience. When we act upon His obedience and see the fruit that comes from it, we then are more willing to make grander strides to seek and obey Him because we trust Him. As a believer, I need to surrender that control over to the Lord, knowing He is going to work everything out for His good and not our own. I pray that you do the same.

Who, Me?

Being obedient doesn't always come naturally. Many times, it takes an enormous amount of effort just to take a step of faith, let alone a leap. One verse in scripture that has helped me tremendously when battling with doubts and uncertainty is about a mustard seed. Ring any bells? It says:

"You don't have enough faith," Jesus told them. "I tell you the truth, if you had faith even as small as a mustard seed, you could say to this mountain, 'Move from here to there,' and it would move; and nothing would be impossible for you."

—Matthew 17:20–21 (NLT)

I have memorized this verse time and time again and quote it often. What is so fascinating about mustard seeds is that they are a whopping two millimeters in diameter. That is about the size of the tip of a crayon. Since they are relatively small, why does God want us to have that kind of faith? I believe that God can work wonders through His people. The great thing is that God doesn't demand huge amounts of faith to do what He commands. The only faith He requires is the faith of a mustard seed. Once that tiny seed of faith is planted, the Lord will increase that faith as you walk His path of obedience. Having a mustard seed type of faith may seem easy, but let me tell you a time when having faith in the unknown was a battle for me.

I already mentioned that I worked at a youth camp called Snowbird Wilderness Outfitters in North Carolina, but I never told you how I got to that point in my life. Growing up, my youth pastor took several students, one week over the summer, to this Christian camp in the mountains. I was never one to really leave home alone, so I hesitated about going for a long time. I was fearful about what could happen being away for that long and so far away from my home in Florida. One day, my youth pastor asked me, "Are you going to camp with us this year?" Before I responded, I could see he saw the uncertainty on my face. All of a sudden, he went to his office, pulled out a shirt, threw it at me, and said, "Be here Monday morning at 4:00 a.m. You are going to SWO."

I honestly didn't know what to say or do after that. I was beyond shocked! Most teenagers and young adults would love to get away from their parents and hometowns for a week, but not me. The week leading up to Monday seemed to drag on. The closer the departure day was, the more scared and nervous I became. From the stories I had heard, I didn't feel right about going. My stomach was all in knots, and I wanted nothing more than for this to be a dream. Nervous or not, I woke up at 3:30 a.m., along with my mom, who drove me to the church. I wanted this trip to end before it even began.

One great thing about SWO is that they assign staff members to be with your church group all week long to really be intentional and invest in the students. Being that I was twenty at the time, I got to talk with the counselors one-on-one quite a lot. One afternoon during recreation, I remember sitting at the pool and talking with a staff member about my week. As we sat on the side of the pool with our feet dangling in the water, out of nowhere she asked if I would ever consider working there. My first reaction was "Absolutely not!" However, when I got on the bus to come home, the Lord spoke to my heart. His voice was loud and it was clear. He said, *Sierra, I want you to apply to work at Snowbird next year.*

My heart immediately sank. I couldn't work at Snowbird! There was a reason why the words *comfort zone* were a big part of my vocabulary at the time. Don't get me wrong; I loved going as a camper. It was easy, with no responsibilities or strings attached. Working on staff, however, seemed way out of my element. The SWO staff participated in skits (I'm not a theater gal); they had to run recreation (which I had no idea how to do); I would be away from my hometown for three months; I only knew one or two people who worked there regularly, and I didn't know how to share the Gospel or teach people about the Bible at all (a major task). Need I say more? I was a wreck, to say the least.

Day after day, I kept making excuses for myself as to why I shouldn't apply for summer staff in 2016. Once I saw how tedious and taxing the application was, that really did me in. My mom honestly didn't think I would apply. She just nodded her head as if to say, "I'll believe it when I see it."

However, God had different plans and really put a desire in my heart to at least apply and see what would happen.

Little did I know that one small step of obedience could lead me to a peaceful and joyous outcome. Needless to say, I got the job, and that was the best summer of my life! I grew so much in my faith as a believer! I made long-lasting friendships; I never got sick (it is never fun when you get sick away from home), grew in my self-esteem, and was able to teach students about the Lord and invest in their lives for three summers afterward, while also staying a year to work as an intern.

Although the outcome was better than I had imagined, it was all because I had faith and obeyed the Lord. I had a mustard seed kind of faith that allowed the Lord to work mightily in my life during that time. He made the impossible possible. Fear of the unknown, I thought, was an enormous obstacle to overcome. So much so that I thought it was impossible. To put it bluntly, the fear about applying for the job didn't go away, but the strength that God gave me grew to conquer that fear. Writing and publishing this book was even a challenge for me to overcome. Knowing that numerous people would read parts of my story was frightening. *Will people actually read my book? What will my friends and family think of me after they read it? Did I say all God wanted me to?* Although my fear was heightening, I knew that the outcome of abundant peace and joy would be better than the present moment of anxiety. God had called me to this opportunity. Therefore, I was going to take full advantage of it, knowing that He is in control from the very beginning.

Just because God calls you to something doesn't mean that fear and doubt don't exist. Anything new and uncertain is scary. Even change can be difficult. I used to hate change, even the idea of it. I soon came to realize that without change, you can't grow. Since I stepped out of my comfort zone and chose His path of obedience, God grew me and my faith radically, like never before! It was evident in the way I lived my life, the way I spoke to people, and the way I carried myself. The enemy is crafty, and he will use anything to make you doubt, fear, and question God's call and direction for your life. However, don't let fear make you miss out on the life God has for you. The Lord puts His power in us to do His will. Isn't that refreshing? If you have Christ in your heart, you better believe that He is going to call you to do some life-changing things for His Kingdom! It all starts with God's voice, your choice, and a tiny seed of faith.

What are some times where you displayed a mustard seed kind of faith in your own life?

How Should You Obey?

Faith over Fear

God uses the words "do not fear" 365 times in the Bible. He knew that people fear a lot. I know I do. I guess that's why there is one for every day of the year. Actually, one of the biggest battles I have ever had to face is fighting fear and anxiety. Now, I am not going to say that it has been an easy road for me or that my coping mechanisms will work for you, but I encourage you to share what you are going through with others. No one likes to feel lonely, ashamed, unloved, or abandoned. That is exactly what road fear and anxiety can take you down, a path of destruction. That's where I was heading. Yet when you turn away from that path and get on God's path,

He will definitely make a way for you to become a stronger, more confident person because you are living for Him and not a slave to fear and anxiety any longer. Hold on to this promise: you are not alone.

Stay alert! Watch out for your great enemy, the devil. He prowls around like a roaring lion, looking for someone to devour. Stand firm against him, and be strong in your faith. Remember that your family of believers all over the world is going through the same kind of suffering you are.

—1 Peter 5:8–9 (NLT)

Don't get me wrong, I still deal with anxiety and fear to this day, but because I let God take control from the beginning, I have learned to trust in Him whenever those lies try to take me down. Let me explain. I remember my very first panic attack. I was in middle school, I'd say about seventh grade, and I was having a sleepover with my two cousins at my granny's house. Now, if you have ever had a sleepover, you know that fun is involved. We watched our favorite movies, ate our favorite snack (which was always ice cream), and laughed and giggled at one another until our sides were sore. All was going well until bedtime.

My granny slept with my youngest cousin in the back bedroom of her house, while my other cousin and I slept in another bedroom close by. Like we normally do at a sleepover, we didn't just go to bed right away. My cousin and I usually talked until we fell asleep. Well, both of us got into bed and lay there talking for what seemed to be about twenty minutes. Then, all of a sudden, I sat straight up in bed. Honestly, I don't know what came over me. My cousin called my name several times to see if I was okay, but I couldn't speak to her. It was like my ability to speak was gone. She ran out of the room and got our granny. Now, by this time my heart was pounding out of my chest, I was covered in sweat, and I felt like I couldn't breathe. To be completely honest, I felt like I was going to die, and there was nothing I or anyone could do about it. I was so anxious! My granny rushed me to my house and called the paramedics. They quickly arrived and checked everything out. Turns out I was fine. I just experienced my first panic attack, and it was a scary thing for sure. The crazy thing is that nothing brought it on. After that night, I tried to recollect the things that were bothering me to make me so anxious. Something in my life had to have triggered that panic attack. In the days following the episode, I began thinking, but nothing came to mind. What did I have to worry about?

    I get it. Some families have issues with anxiety, and the lineage can trickle down onto you. There are a few people in my family that can attest to this. Nothing in my life that I knew of had brought that first attack on all those years ago. Yet something in my life was not right. Shortly after, I began to question God and let this fear rattle and overtake me. Where did my hope lie? Why was this happening to me? I thought that being anxious and having panic attacks was uncontrollable. Now, this might be the case for some people, and I don't want to undermine that. But although you might struggle with crippling anxiety, that doesn't mean you have to stay there. After all, fear doesn't control me and you, God does. Honestly, it took almost a year to truly understand and enforce coping mechanisms that would help me during these difficult times. I'll share more of that as you continue reading. If this is a struggle or becoming one for you, don't let fear and anxiety make you miss out on the life you were born to live. Be a warrior, not a worrier. Fight your worries and fears with the power of the Holy Spirit and

His Word. You make the choice. You get to choose your thoughts. You get to choose your responses. You get to choose to take action over your life.

One of the strongest things you can do is ask for help. So if you need help, ask for it. Why? Because you are acknowledging that you need it and want to try to correct the challenges you are facing. God has given each of us a brain, so use it. Because I face anxiety doesn't mean that I am exempt from battling depression. One can bounce off the other. At one point in my life, I thought this world would be better off without me. That was another lie from the pit of Hell. I knew that I needed help in confronting this spiritual battle. It was hard opening up about it, but I had come to realize that keeping the struggle in would only make it worse. That is what the enemy wants you to do, hide your pain from the rest of the world. He wants you to let it fester and drag you down deeper into a bottomless pit where there is no escape. Without me admitting to myself and others that I needed help, there was no way out. Once I did, it felt like a huge weight had been lifted. I then was able to get the help I so desperately needed. God made us for community. He wants us to share our struggles and imperfections with one another. By opening up and being vulnerable, it might prompt others to share their struggles too. There is absolutely no shame in asking for help. It takes a lot of guts, in my opinion. Don't go at this alone. Don't stay in that rut. Tell someone, anyone, about the issues in your life.

Is there something in your own life that is taking you captive?

Who do you think would be a person you can open up to about this struggle?

[Satan] is a liar and the father of lies.

—John 8:44 (NLT)

I heard this saying on the radio: "The enemy will tell you anything that you are willing to believe about yourself." That is 100 percent true. He knows the tricks and will do anything to tangle you into his web of lies. Here are a few examples:

The enemy says no one loves you, but God says, "I died because of My love for you" (Romans 5:8; Jeremiah 13:3).

The enemy says you are not good enough, but God says that "you are fearfully and wonderfully made" with a purpose (Psalm 139:13–16; Galatians 1:15).

The enemy says that no one understands you, but God understands all (Hebrews 4:15–16; Psalm 139:1–12).

The enemy wants you to keep your struggles hidden, but God wants you to bring your struggles to the light (Ephesians 5:11; Hebrews 4:13).

The enemy says that no one cares about you, but God says that you are valued (Matthew 6:25–34).

The enemy will say that you can't get through this, but God will provide a way out (1 Corinthians 10:13).

The enemy says that you are fighting your battles alone, but God says, "I will never leave you nor forsake you" (Deuteronomy 31:6).

No matter what stage of life you are going through, the enemy will tell you lies. That's a given. He is a deceiver and wants to get you to your lowest point. However, it is up to you whether you believe the lies or not and stay in that pit of despair. Always remember that you were made to feel loved, accepted, and encouraged by God no matter the struggle you are facing.

What lies do you believe about yourself?

How can you overshadow those lies with God's truth?

Prayer

You may not know how to obey the Lord and what He has called you to. You may not know where to start or the right direction to go to get you on the right path. My go-to whenever I am lost is prayer. Praying to God is vital in your relationship with Him. If you want to know what He wants you to do, you have to put forth effort into the relationship. Having a conversation with God should be the easiest thing we can ever do. I can assure you, talking to Him daily will allow you to grow more confident with the plans He has for you.

You might find this comforting: there's no right or wrong way to do it. You don't have to use large vocabulary to impress God. You don't have to be scared about telling Him the hard things (He made you, so nothing surprises Him). It doesn't even matter the time of day you pray. What matters is that you are sharing your heart fully with Him. Vulnerability can be challenging in any relationship. With God, however, He wants to help you with the mess. He wants to fix the entangled roots of bondage. He wants to comfort you in times of need. He wants to uplift you and give you a peace that only He can provide. In order for you to grow and for Him to work, you need to be vulnerable. So share the mess. Share the fear and uncertainties. Share your problems. Even share your joys. Although it might take days, weeks, or even months, praying to God about your life will give you more insight on where God wants you to go in your life.

Why do you think it is so important to pray to God?

How often do you pray?

Be in the Word

One of the greatest acronyms that I've ever heard is BIBLE:
Basic
Instructions
Before
Leaving
Earth

The Bible is the Book about God, plain and simple. It tells what happened in His time and how things were done. We can see how people went through different trials and obstacles. Since we are not in Biblical times any more, we can still learn a great deal about life. Reading scripture can take you on a beautiful journey! Since the Bible is historical, it talks about people's real struggles, trials, and joys they faced. It unpacks how they managed to lean on God or go the opposite direction altogether. Numerous life lessons can be taught just by opening this Book and intentionally studying its pages. While Christians communicate with God through prayer, God communicates with His people through the Bible. We can't know what to do in this life apart from His Word. When you're not diving into scripture, it is very hard to hear God's voice. The Bible gives us instructions on how to act, as well as how to obey, in this world. It instructs us to love one another, provides clarity when battling temptation, and brings conviction upon us when we need it most.

2 Timothy 3:16–17 clearly states that the Bible is a guidebook for our lives. This verse says that the Bible is an inspiration. In my study Bible, inspiration means "God breathed." From this we know that the author of the Bible is God. Therefore, we know that the scriptures are legit and authoritative because they were written and made by God Himself.

There are four ways that the Bible can be studied. These ways are all useful to help us in our daily life. The first is doctrine. The word doctrine means to teach. Acts 2:42 is a great example of this. New believers devote themselves to the teaching of the apostles. Since the apostles saw Jesus firsthand, the people knew that what they were saying was the truth. Today, we haven't literally seen or heard Jesus in the flesh. Nevertheless, He lives inside of us (Christians) by the Holy Spirit and uses us to be an example to others, which, in turn, points people to Him.

Secondly, we have reproof. The internet's definition of reproof is the expression of blame. With that being said, conviction is born. Conviction happens when you are guilty of something. John 16:8 states that God will come to convict the world. For example, picture a student that cheated on a test. Maybe she didn't study or forgot to altogether. Whatever the reason, she came home after that day at school and couldn't sleep. All she could think about was the test and how she was not honest in completing it. After a week, she finally went to the teacher and confessed what she had done. Yes, there were consequences for her action, but a relief came over her.

She was glad that she came clean. If you think about it, it is the same thing with our lives. When we know something is wrong and we do it anyway, that brings conviction. The Holy Spirit should convict us. If you don't feel that conviction, I encourage you to reevaluate your life. God wants us to be convicted so we can mature and grow in Him. Conviction is a good thing. Without it, Christians are no better than we were before we believed.

The third way the Bible can be studied is by correction. Think about when you were young and did something not pleasing to your parents. They might have put you in time-out or spanked you. Either way, it was a consequence. If you think about it, when Christians do wrong, God punishes us. Just because He punishes us doesn't mean He doesn't love us anymore. It is the complete opposite. God loves you and wants the best for you. Therefore, He has consequences for your actions because He wants better for you. In 2 Timothy 2:15, it states that the scriptures will make you wise. Also, Proverbs 6:23 says that the reproofs of discipline are ways of life. God helps us know what is right and wrong by reading scripture. It provides directions that will assist us in our walk of life.

Instruction is the last way the Bible can be studied. We are to listen and accept instruction, according to Proverbs 19:20. Also, Proverbs 8:33 says that we shouldn't ignore God's instruction for our lives. The only way to know His instruction is by reading and meditating on scripture. It doesn't just show us what we need to do in some or most areas of our life but in all areas of our life. Whenever I hear the word "instructions," a child comes to mind. When children are young, they need instructions so they don't get out of hand. The Bible says that if we train up a child in the way they should go, they will not depart from it, according to Proverbs 22:6. We are a child in the eyes of Christ. We need to submit to the authority of scripture so that we can learn and become mature in our daily walk with the Lord.

The enemy is sneaky and is trying desperately to get us out of the Word and into the world by any tactics possible. This world, as well as our fleshly desires and emotions, will lead us astray and ultimately fail us. Because of this, we shouldn't base the truth on our feelings or the world's standards but on the truths that come from God and His unchanging Word. Knowing scripture is the only truth we have in our world. That's why there are so many scripture references in this book. I want you to seek the truth for yourself in the Word of God. You can't bring glory to someone you don't know. Therefore, I encourage you to spend time in the Word daily. You will be surprised what God can teach you. Personally, I grab a pencil and paper and really dig deep into His Word by journaling. By doing this, He speaks to my heart more intently and allows me to grow and mature in Him each day. Also, I pray hard and try to block out all distractions that may hinder my quiet time. When I study in depth, God shows me things and allows me to be convicted more when I write my thoughts down. That way, I can plainly see where I have to grow more in my walk with Him.

If you don't know where to begin, that's okay. Proverbs is always a great book to start. It has thirty-one chapters for thirty-one days in a month. On the first day of the month, read the first chapter. Second day, read chapter two, and so on. I usually start with the book of James or Philippians. Each person has a different approach to studying the Bible, and that is okay. Find what works best for you. If you don't have a desire to read scripture, pray that you do. Ask God where He wants you, and go from there. Go at your own pace. Dive into scripture with an open mind and heart. Let God direct and guide your life through His living and active Word. I promise, God will speak to you, but you have to be willing to listen.

Here are some study tools to help you get started:

1. What does this passage say about God?
2. What does this passage say about man (me)?
3. In this passage, is there any sin to confess or avoid?
4. In this passage, is there a rule to follow or command to obey?
5. How do I respond and follow in obedience?

It is one thing to read scripture, but application is key. God wants us to live out our faith. In order to do that, we have to intentionally seek Him by prayer and Bible reading and not just check it off our to-do list. Although you may read the Bible, it does you no good unless you actually memorize scripture and apply what you read. What are you getting out of it? How is that impacting your life? God wants you to be radically changed by scripture. As mentioned, He knows your heart and the desires that flow from it. Just simply knowing scripture won't suffice. Application of scripture, though, will impact your life drastically as you continue to grow in the Lord.

Is reading the Bible important to you? Why or why not?

Why isn't reading scripture enough? Why should you apply what you read?

Confidently Obey

Don't worry about how to respond or what to say. God will give you the right words at the right time. For it is not you who will be speaking—it will be the Spirit of your Father speaking through you.

—Matthew 10:19–20 (NLT)

When I applied to work at camp, the main thing that scared me was the fact that I would be sharing the Gospel with other people. Now, I had never been one to openly share my faith before I applied, so it became a sudden fear that was hard to overcome. My main concern was that most of the kids that came to SWO grew up in church, so they'd heard the Gospel being presented all of their life. They knew all the "churchy" answers and the children's stories like Jonah and the Whale and David and Goliath. My initial thought was, *Since they have been going to church their whole life, would they really listen to me—a college student?* It was also apparent that some students had never heard the Gospel before, and frankly, they didn't care to hear it. It quickly occurred to me that all they wanted was a week away from their parents and a teenage playground to have adventures with their friends. My confidence was steadily depleting while my nerves were quickly heightening as this played out in my mind.

Before the campers went to bed each night, they had a gathering time called share groups. These groups (usually split by gender and age) focused on their day, the messages that were being presented, and the hard questions the kids felt they needed to ask. Primarily, though, share groups were a time to unpack the messages at a deeper level to help the students internalize and personalize it into their own life. The first time I ever led share groups, I had about six eighth-grade girls and a coleader who was with me. Going into it, neither of us had never led a group before, so we didn't really know what to expect. No lie, it was awkward silence for the first ten minutes. With their notebooks flipped open, I could see that most of the girls seemed to draw during the messages rather than listen to them. The coleader and I proceeded to ask questions to the group, go over the schedule for the next day, and ask the students if they needed to talk one-on-one for a specific reason. None of them felt obligated, so we dismissed, and the girls all ran to shower to get ready for bed. This continued all week long. Needless to say, they didn't have a big interest in share groups.

Honestly, this left me feeling like I didn't do my job. My confidence was now shattered. God had called me to this camp to help students grow in their walk with the Lord. Yet it seemed like the girls could care less about the sermons but mainly prioritized the free time and the adventurous recreational activities. They really didn't engage in conversation, and this led me to overthink and analyze. *Why aren't they talking with us? Am I coming across too harsh or too gentle with my questioning? Am I doing enough? Do they realize how much I care for their spiritual growth?* To be honest, that share group was the shortest one out of my whole summer that year, lasting a whole twenty minutes! (Did I mention the first ten that we sat in awkward silence?)

Ashley, who I mentioned in a previous chapter, could see that I was struggling. She then managed to pull me aside one night and talk about the problem I was having. I explained to her that I thought I wasn't doing a "good enough" job while in share groups. She could tell my focus was drifting, so she quickly said something that I will never forget. She said, "Sierra, your job isn't to make them listen or care; your only job is to be obedient to the Lord." That stuck with me to this day. Granted, it was disappointing to lead share groups and for there to be no change of heart or big decision being made. However, I had been looking at the reactions of obedience instead of the actions of obedience. Ashley reminded me that my only objective was to be obedient to the Lord. I honored that by submitting my application, which got me to work at camp in the first place. I couldn't hit the students over the head with the Bible in order for them to understand the Gospel and become saved. The change of heart had to be made by the Lord, not by me. I simply had to let God take control and nudge the individual student Himself. I couldn't do anything to make that happen; I could only help the process by reiterating what was already being mentioned in the sermon.

I planted the seed in your hearts, and Apollos watered it, but it was God who made it grow. It is not important who does the planting, or who does the watering. What's important is that God makes the seed grow.
—*1 Corinthians 3:6–8 (NLT)*

When a person plants a seed, someone has to come along and actually plant it into the soil. Once it's planted, people can come to nurture it and help it grow. Share groups were those times. The girls had already heard the message being taught by the speaker. Therefore, the seed was already planted in their hearts. As a counselor, it was my job to cultivate that seed. I couldn't control how fast the seed grew, but I could control how much I watered and tended to it. In order to do that, I needed to build relationships with them while also encouraging them and investing in their spiritual lives for that week of camp. My only hope was that they went home desiring God more than when they first arrived.

In the book of Ezekiel, God is talking to Ezekiel in a dream. In this dream, God gave him a specific job. Ezekiel's task was to go to Israel, a land of stubborn and hardheaded people, and deliver the Gospel message. God said, "Even though they are stubborn and probably won't listen, go and tell anyway." That is exactly what the Lord was calling me to do. Even though the students didn't want to participate or have any interest in group discussion, it was still my job to help direct and encourage them during that time. God knew the task was going to be challenging. He knew the outcome being presented was hard. He knew the intent of the student's heart and their willingness to listen to His message. He knew my frustrations and issues before they even occurred. He could see how much I cared for these girls. My heart ached for them and the effort they were putting in. I only needed to be concerned with my job—being a vessel that the Lord could use to speak His message during share groups.

Being obedient isn't necessarily the easiest thing to do—especially if what you are doing isn't playing out the way you want it to. As you just read, the outcome I experienced was far from what I thought it would actually turn out to be. Nevertheless, I was obedient to the Lord in my actions and my words. It didn't matter if the kids came to repentance—it was not my job to make them care. It didn't matter that the kids didn't ask any questions or stay after to talk—it was not my job to make them. Even the length of the share group didn't matter—it was not my job to have the longest share group. God already knew the outcome. What truly mattered was that I was used at that moment in time for a specific reason: to be a mouthpiece for the Lord.

Whenever you are faced with a similar situation, I encourage you to think about why you are doing what you are doing. Are you doing it to get a certain reaction out of someone? Are you doing it to make others jealous? Are you doing it to get noticed? Consequently, are you doing it to fulfill God's call? Don't sweat the small stuff. The feelings that you have going through the task may be valid, but how does God feel about your act of obedience? That's the ultimate question that truly matters. As much as you might want to be the hero and save people, that is not your job. It's God's. Your job is to be a representation of Christ. By doing this, others may come to know Him simply because of your actions. Be confident in the fact that God has placed you where He wants you for a reason. He has called you to do a significant task that only you can accomplish. As believers, we have a responsibility to obtain whether people listen to us or not. Let that be a motivator and confidence booster as you navigate the road of obedience.

What are some steps you can take to show that you are confident in the Lord?

Are you letting people's opinions (or your own opinion) affect your obedience to the Lord? If so, how can you stop it?

When Should You Obey?

Instant Obedience

As I have stated before, the enemy loves to make us doubt the plan God has for us. Although doubt can have a negative effect on us, God wants instant obedience from His children. I mean, just look at our world today. Simple things like cooking your food, shopping online, or paying your bills can all be done in an instant. You use a microwave to cook your food in less than a minute. You browse your computer looking for clothing or the latest gadget that you want, pay with your credit card, and then it is at your doorstep within a matter of days. I mean, sometimes I get angry when I have to wait in the drive-thru for more than ten minutes. Can you see where I am going with this? Our world wants instant gratification. I mean, we even have instant gravy, mashed potatoes, and grits, for crying out loud! No one wants to wait. I don't like waiting, and I'm sure you don't either.

Do you consider yourself a patient person? Why or why not?

God, though, is very patient with His children. Yet when He calls us to do something, I, a lot of times, put it off. *Does God really want to me to do this? I'll just wait a couple of days and pray about it.* I am guilty of this all the time. When God calls us to obey Him, He isn't saying, obey Me when you're ready. We might never be fully ready to obey the Lord. God is saying, I am ready for you to obey Me now. He is calling us to obey even when we don't feel equipped. God will empower you with His power no matter the job. One of my life sayings that I heard at camp is "God doesn't call the qualified, but He qualifies the called." No hesitation. No doubt. No excuses.

One of the many Bible stories that have to do with obedience is the story of Jonah. Some may know the story, but let me give a recap for those who don't. God gave a message to Jonah, "Get up and go to Nineveh. Tell the people there about Me, or else this place and all its people will be destroyed, for they are being very sinful and wicked." Now, this might seem like a simple task. God spoke, Jonah goes and tells the people about Jesus, people get saved, and all is well. You see, Jonah was a man who was very prideful. He really didn't want to be obedient, because he didn't want to see the people of Nineveh change. Their hearts were very worldly and destructive, and Jonah wanted them to stay that way. He wanted them to suffer because he hated them. He had a "you made your bed; now you have to lie in it" type of attitude.

Well, Jonah got up and went, all right. He went completely in the opposite direction God told him to go. He purchased a ticket and set sail to a place called Tarshish. By doing this, Jonah was hoping to escape the Lord. How do you think that played out?

While sailing on this boat, a raging storm soon appeared. Everyone, of course, was terrified! Winds became violent. Waves got larger and larger in size, threatening the boat and endangering all of its passengers. The crew members tried everything they knew of to lighten the load of the ship. They began throwing cargo left and right into the sea, hoping this would help the ship stay afloat. Nothing seemed to work, and the captain and passengers grew more frantic by the second. The captain then went below deck and spotted Jonah asleep. "Get up!" said the captain. "And pray to your god that he will spare us."

By this time, the crew began seriously questioning, "Why is this happening to us? What made this violent storm suddenly appear?" The storm was getting bigger by the minute!

"I already told you that I am running from the Lord," Jonah replied. "It's my fault. Throw me into the sea, and I am certain that the storm will stop." Without hesitation, the crew did as Jonah said. They tossed him into the sea. Immediately, the storm ceased. The waves and the wind grew faint. Everything was still. Everyone on the ship was so in awe of the Lord's great power that they vowed to serve Him forevermore.

Now by this time, the sea was calm, the crew members confessed their need for a Savior, and Jonah admitted to going against the Lord. All was good, right? Not even close. When Jonah was thrown into the ocean, a huge fish swallowed him! That's right. Jonah was in the belly of a whale for three days and three nights. Obviously, the Lord had intended for this to happen. Just imagine the smells he would smell of rotting fish and waste. Imagine the sounds he would hear, water motioning in and out of the belly, or maybe not even a single motion, just extremely quiet and silent. Imagine the darkness he would face all within the belly of this enormous whale. He was alone, alone with only his thoughts. This gave Jonah a lot of time to think and a lot of time to pray. He sought the Lord during this time; passionately and sincerely.

I cried out to the Lord in my great trouble and He answered me.
—*Jonah 2:2 (NLT)*

You, O Lord my God, snatched me from the jaws of death! As my life was slipping away, I remembered the Lord.
—*Jonah 2:6–7 (NLT)*

The Lord must have heard Jonah's cry. He soon allowed the whale to spit Jonah out onto the beach. Jonah's prayers were answered! Now, the Lord told Jonah to go to Nineveh again. Do you think he listened this time? Although he wasn't happy about it, Jonah did as the Lord told him. Being that he did as the Lord commanded, the Lord spared the people and the town from its detriment. They were all saved because Jonah listened and obeyed the Lord.

Like I mentioned in previous chapters, serving and obeying the Lord just doesn't affect you; it affects others around you. Take Jonah's story, for instance. He could have saved so many people so much time and heartache if he would have simply obeyed the Lord from the very beginning. He put all the crew members and captain in grave danger all because of his selfishness. All that time Jonah was trying to escape the Lord, the people of Nineveh could have gotten saved earlier and could point more people to Christ in that time frame. As stated, obedience isn't optional. The Lord's plan is going to work out whether you like it or not. There is no sense in running, trying to avoid it, or taking the safe way out. If you do, you might get swallowed by a whale, figuratively of course. Obey instantly, knowing and trusting that the Lord will use you for His glory no matter the path that you are on.

Do you find it hard to obey the Lord when He calls you to do something?

What makes you so hesitant?

Selfishness vs. Selflessness

Answer me this: When is it a good time to be selfish?

The obvious answer is "never." It is never a good idea to become selfish. I personally believe that selfishness is the root of every sin we commit. Think about it. Lust of the eyes: we want to look at something enticing. Lust of the flesh: we give in to our sinful desires. The pride of life: no one comes before me. I have it all and need no one to convince me otherwise. The three deadly sins, they are all intertwined with selfishness.

Convenience and selfishness go well together too. Let me give you some examples: *If it isn't too late, I'll do what my parents want. If I have enough money, I'll help them out. If I have time, I'll give them a ride.*

If I. If I. If I. Basically, if it doesn't inconvenience my time, my plans, my activities, then I will sacrifice my time, my money, and my actions for another person. Does that make sense? I'll do what I want, when I want, as long as it benefits me. I could care less about anyone else.

Here's another: *If they apologize first, then I'll apologize back. If they tell the truth, I'll come clean too.*

If they. If they. If they. Like always, I have to look out for #1 right? I mean, I don't care how my actions hurt others or what people will think of me after the damage is done. If they don't apologize, why should I? If they don't fess up, who cares? Who needs to know? If it doesn't benefit me, it's not worth my time. My friends, this is totally the wrong mindset to have!

This part of the book could have been clumped into "How Do You Obey?" but I wanted to show this side of Jonah. As I previously mentioned, Jonah was indeed selfish even after he was spit out by that whale. He went to Nineveh, as the Lord wanted him to; however, he was still angry. Although his actions may not have been self-centered, his attitude sure was. Since God had shown favor and forgiveness to the people of Nineveh, this made Jonah furious! He wanted them to wallow in their mistakes and self-indulging ways. Well, God didn't stand for it and forgave them.

Jonah wasn't about to forgive all those wicked people, so why should God? Selfishness became apparent, and Jonah started complaining to the Lord. "I knew this would happen!" he said. "I knew you would forgive them and be a merciful God." He complained time and time again. Jonah stated that he would rather die than to have these people know the Lord. Talk about being selfish! Jonah then decided to wait it out and see what would happen. I mean, since he took out all of his complaints to the Lord, the Lord was sure to give him what he wanted, right? (Wrong!) So he found a spot on the side of the city gates and decided to wallow in self-pity.

While he was doing so, the Lord arranged for a plant to grow, shading Jonah from the sweltering sun. This relieved him from some discomfort, and he was very grateful for the plant the Lord had provided. The next morning, though, a worm came and ate through the plant, causing it to wither away and eventually die. Now Jonah had no shade, still felt very angry and discontent, and wished death upon himself. God merely questioned Jonah. To put it directly, the Lord said, "You mean to tell me that you are angry that the plant died which kept you cool. Yet more than 120,000 people in Nineveh are living in spiritual darkness, and you don't want me to show compassion to them?"

Then He said to the crowd, "If any of you wants to be my follower, you must give up (turn from) your own way, take up your cross daily, and follow me."
—Luke 9:23 (NLT)

Selfishness was the root of Jonah's sin. We don't know what actually became of Jonah after that, but we do know that he would rather have died than to have God be merciful on those he hated. Jonah was only concerned with how he felt about the people. He had no consideration for their spiritual growth or individual choices. He was only focused on himself for himself. He had no concern for the spiritual well-being of others.

In the verse stated above, the word *"turn"* means to change direction. One is changing their self from selfish to selfless. I personally believe that the only way to become selfless is to give yourself wholeheartedly to the One who is never selfish. Being a Christian means that God isn't fitting into your plan, but you're fitting into His (Philippians 2:12–13). This is a daily submission and requires work, not just when we feel like it. Jonah was so fixated on getting what he wanted, not what the people deserved. He was only thinking about himself and not the thousands of people involved. He wasn't focused on the big picture God was painting. Jonah only saw the here and now. Anger then became evident because he wanted things done his way. Christianity doesn't work like that. Yes, things may go askew, but God has a rhyme and a reason behind anything and everything you and I may ever face. By putting selfishness aside and fully committing to the plan God has for us, our attitudes and our actions will show the light of Christ even though our plan may seem discombobulated. Selfishness starts to dwindle when we look at ourselves less and others more. The more we are concentrating on God and His people, the more we will be like the Lord. When we become more selfless, we are willing to do whatever it takes to win hearts for Christ.

What are some steps you can take in your own life to become selfless instead of selfish?

Where Is God Calling You to Obey?

Go, therefore, and make disciples of all nations, baptizing them in the name of the Father, and of the Son, and of the Holy Spirit, teaching them to observe all that I have commanded you. And behold, I am with you always, to the end of the age.

—Matthew 28:19–20 (ESV)

The first word to begin these verses is the word "*go.*" Now, "*go*" is considered to be a verb. It shows action, meaning to leave, depart, and travel from one place to another. It is insinuating that people need to get up and go to their destination. Whatever our choice of transportation, God wants us to go to the destination He has called us to. He will provide the tools needed, but only if we obey. God is sending us, His people, to do His work. It is not a choice but a command. We are commanded to go and tell others about Him, no ifs, ands, or buts.

Joshua was faced with this problem in the Bible. Moses, the Israelite leader, died. God then called to Joshua and said, "I want you to lead my people (the Israelites) into the Promised Land." I'm sure Joshua's first reaction was to question God. After all, he was taking the place of Moses (the person who had been leading them from the beginning). Joshua's nerves and anxieties about the whole thing were very real and a tough pill to swallow. Yet God already knew the game plan and had the steps in place to make it happen. Since Joshua was afraid and quite discouraged about this upcoming journey, God reassures him three times by saying, "Be strong and courageous" (Joshua 1:6, 1:7, and 1:9).

This is my command—be strong and courageous. Do not be afraid or discouraged. For the Lord your God is with you wherever you go.

—Joshua 1:9 (NLT)

You might be asking yourself, "Where does God want me to go?" A question that most people ask in their lifetime. Let me just say that it is okay to not know every detail of your life. It is okay to not know where you are going. I've been there myself. The reality is that we won't get to see the big pictures as God does. That is where trust comes into play. Regardless of the destination, and despite your apprehensiveness on the subject, God directs and instructs us to go, wherever that may be. These three places that I'm about to mention will hopefully give you a glimpse of where you can obey the Lord.

Overseas

I've known numerous people that go overseas and share the Gospel with others. This is a wonderful experience that is nothing short of God-ordained. I believe that the Lord puts this strong calling on an individual's heart. Not to say that ministering overseas is more important than ministering in the States, but I strongly believe that serving overseas is a true blessing and testing of one's faith. Consider the various obstacles. You are thousands of miles away from the people that you love; there might be a language barrier you have to encounter, and some obvious obstacles like travel expenses and navigation once you're there might be a challenge. Going to a new place, especially overseas, can be a culture shock to a lot of people too. If you think you are being called to go overseas, great! Continue to pray and seek the Lord for the answer. If God wants you to go, He will prepare and equip you with everything you need to do His work from the beginning to the end.

New State

My time in North Carolina was one I will treasure forever! I didn't get there of my own accord, though. I sought the will of God in order for me to know where He wanted me to go after graduation. Mind you, He grew my faith immensely during my time there. God knew that it was a big leap of faith on my part. Therefore, once I jumped in feet-first, He honored that by forming deep friendships, increasing my confidence, and growing my relationship deeper with Him. If you seek the Lord and go where He sees fit, He will honor that by rewarding you in due time.

In Your Own Backyard

Although going overseas or moving to a new state is exciting, not all people are called to live that kind of life. You don't have to go far in order to obey God. No matter where He has placed you, though, faith in God does require some type of discomfort. If you believe in God, He is calling you to go out of your comfort zone. Like Louie Giglio says, "In order to grow in Christ more, you have to become comfortable with the uncomfortable." God wants to challenge you, mold you, and grow you. He wants us out of our comfort zones in order for us to rely solely on Him.

God sees the heart in each individual person. Therefore, comfort zones will vary depending on each person's heart. What may be easy for some people may be extremely uncomfortable for others to achieve. For example, some people might be scared to go next door and share the Gospel with their neighbors out of fear of rejection. Others may have no fear and can boldly proclaim Christ whenever and wherever the chance arises.

Whatever the case, God knows the intent and the initiative behind your actions. So take a risk, knowing the Lord will empower you through it.

It can be easy to compare yourself to other people during this process. The opportunities God has given you may be different from what God has equipped your friends and family for. That's perfectly okay. Always remember that you are your own person, created uniquely by God. It may take a lot of soul-searching, faith-seeking, and risk-taking, but God will use you mightily if you seize the opportunity and step out in obedience.

The saying "Bloom where you are planted" is something that my pastor says a lot. There are many things you can do to obey and serve God right in your own community. Get involved in your local church, start a Bible study, or show hospitality to your neighbors. Depending on the task, it may take a giant leap on your part to do what God has instructed. Maybe you are not happy with where the Lord has you right now. Maybe you think you need to do something more exciting than what you are doing. This, my friend, means that you are not content in the Lord. For me, sometimes I think the word contentment means the same thing as the word stagnant. Think of a lake. If the water becomes stagnant, there is no ebb and flow to the water. It is only staying still, not moving or going anywhere, making the lake possibly infested with diseases. Being stagnant means that you are doing nothing to further yourself to be the best you can be. You are just coasting through life, not really enjoying or ultimately living. Here's a reality check: you can be content without becoming stagnant. Contentment means that you are satisfied with where the Lord has placed you (whatever season it may be), yet in this season you are still growing and maturing in the Lord. Let me explain.

My dream is to one day become a wife and a mother. I have always wanted that for myself. I've pictured my wedding day numerous times, and yet it hasn't happened, at least not yet. Waiting can be hard, especially when you are looking forward to something. To be honest, being single has been a struggle for me. Don't get me wrong; I've always loved the idea of becoming a wife and a mother one day, but I truly didn't think that I would be in this season of singleness for so long. Sometimes I have moments of loneliness and wish I had a husband to do life with. Despite my wants, the Lord hasn't felt a need to bless me with a husband and kids right now, and that is perfectly okay. During this season, though, I have had to find contentment in the Lord rather than my circumstances, which sometimes can be hard. However, just because you are in a waiting season does not mean you have to waste time. Instead, be productive.

I've come to realize that God has allowed me to do things I necessarily wouldn't be able to do if I were married with children. For example, having children and a spouse are both huge blessings, but you then have to consider their wants and needs before your own when making decisions (1 Corinthians 7:32–35). Because of this, I am thankful to God for the opportunities He can give me to serve without having someone else to consider. Whatever season you are in it can be a blessing, but it is up to you to have that mindset. I can assure you that every season we encounter can have its struggles. Singles have different struggles than people who are married, and they have different struggles than parents with kids. The question that I need to ask myself is "Am I still being obedient and content even in this struggling season?" As I approach my thirties, I have a mindset that I am only in this season of singleness once (hopefully). Therefore, how am I glorifying the Lord and making the most of it right now, in the waiting?

Are you content with where the Lord has you?

How are you glorifying the Lord in this season despite your struggle?

Either you are pushing yourself toward the Lord or further away from Him. There is no midpoint. You can be satisfied and still try to pursue something greater. No matter what season of life you are in, there is always a chance for you to grow: to grow in your future goals, become a better version of yourself, and grow your relationship with the Lord. Being satisfied with where the Lord has you is great, but never stop reaching for goals and being the best you can be for Him and yourself.

Don't look back on your life with regret or what ifs. I wish I would have done _____. Don't make excuses as to why you didn't/can't serve the Lord. You only regret the chances you don't take. One thing that I have come to realize is that God isn't concerned with your comfort as much as He is with your holiness toward Him. The more you lean in and trust God in the process of obedience, the more comfortable you will become with where He has you. God is always preparing you for what's next. So be courageous and take initiative now. Don't put off letting God lead your life. Little steps of obedience go a long way. Be obedient in the little things so you can become obedient in the big things too.

What is God calling you to do right now?

What opportunities has God put in your path to serve?

Why Should You Obey?

I wanted to save this question for last because I think it is the most beneficial. Why you obey someone says a lot about you as an individual. Why should you obey your parents? Why should you obey your earthly masters? Most importantly, why should you obey God?

I admit that obeying people on this earth is important and shouldn't be trifled with. However, in this section, I want to solely focus on why we should obey God. You see, if we don't obey the Lord, we are most likely not going to obey the people He has set before us. Here are three reasons that I think we should do just that.

Because You Love God

There is no denying that you need to have faith in God before you can fully love Him. When you have faith, you have complete trust in someone or something. You know that it or they will not let you down, and they or it can protect you and not lead you astray. Faith also means to believe something that is not necessarily based on proof. For example, I think of the movie *A Walk to Remember*. Landon and Jamie had a struggling relationship from the get-go. She was a nice Christian girl who was pure and gentle, while he was the playboy type. Jamie had a huge impact on Landon's life. She made him into a better person simply by her tender yet confident Christian ways. Landon's last lines in the movie were "Jamie saved my life. She taught me everything. About life, hope, and the long journey ahead. I'll always miss her. But our love is like the wind. I can't see it, but I can feel it."

So, can you see the wind? Honest question. If you can, you have very good eyesight. I can't see the wind, but I can see what it does to things. It can tangle hair, knock things over, and blow items away. It is the same thing with Christ and the Holy Spirit. You do not have to see God in order to believe in Him. John 20:29 states that those who have not seen Jesus and still believe in Him will be blessed. Faith is believing in what your eyes cannot see. My eyes can see the sun, but by faith I can see the Son of God. My eyes can see flowers, but by faith I can see the Garden of Eden. My eyes can see mountains, but by faith I can see my God move mountains! Once you have faith in God, only then will you be able to completely and utterly love Him beyond measure.

As mentioned already, in Exodus 20:1-17 it states the commandments of God in the Bible. These commandments were not just a set of rules or restrictions to keep Christians from having fun. I'm sure if you aren't a believer, this may sound ridiculous. Although some may think differently, Christians believe that these rules set by God are for our well-being on this earth. They were made to instruct believers on how to act while we are living among sinful people in a sinful world. Granted we are sinful ourselves. No one is exempt. Therefore, everyone is dealt struggles and strife in their lifetime. Since I have Christ in my heart and promise to love Him above all else, I should want to do everything I can to please and obey Him, starting with the Ten Commandments.

John 14:15 states, "If you love Me, you will keep my commandments." It's as simple as that. In order for you to be obedient to God, you have to have a relationship with Him first. Love is sacrificial. Once you love Jesus enough to surrender your life over to Him, it comes at a cost. No longer are you bound by your own wants and desires, but your love for God should surpass all those things in your life. Since you have that love, you should want to do the things that make God happy (serve others, be obedient, be humble, tell others about Him, etc.). Once you love God, you are able to love the people around you. It should be evident in the way you shine His love upon others by your services and attitude. Although it sometimes seems like a chore, it shouldn't be. I pray that your love for God will deepen and grow stronger as you serve Him both willingly and humbly. If you don't have that relationship, my prayer is that you begin to see His unfathomable and immeasurable love for you. By doing so, my hope is that you will be radically changed for the better when you begin to see yourself through the lens of Christ, truly treasured and beloved.

Do you truly love God the way He should be loved?

Because You Trust God

Trust in the Lord with all your heart. Do not lean on your own understanding. In all your ways acknowledge Him and He will make straight your paths.
—Proverbs 3:5–6 (ESV)

Commit your way to the Lord. Trust in Him and He will act.
—Psalm 37:5 (ESV)

I once heard a story about a tightrope walker. Actually, you may have heard of the man who crossed the Grand Canyon and Niagara Falls on just a tightrope. His nickname is "King of the Wire," but you probably know him best as Nik Wallenda. Nik had been doing stunts that were thrill-seeking for years, although nothing as daredevilish as crossing the Grand Canyon on just a wire. While preparing for his first walk, I am sure that Nik was scared and anxious. Can you imagine the countless hours of practicing and training that went into something like this? He wanted to be sure he was equipped and confident in himself to make this grand trek. After all, his own life was on the line, literally!

Leading up to his grand debut, the media sent out news pages and feeds of this great stunt that was about to take place. News about Nik traveled all over the world. People from all over knew about him and his adventurous ways by the time the event occurred. He was going to be the first person ever to walk the Niagara Falls on a tightrope!

I'm sure a lot of people thought he was crazy for even thinking about this great obstacle, let alone trying to make it happen. When the day of the walk finally came, news and media swarmed the event. Televisions and radios were all on, wanting to capture the moments that Nik Wallenda would soon face. Cameras were flashing as Nik stepped up to begin his stride across 2,200 feet of raging water.

Picture the moment he stepped up to begin. His heart pounding. Palms sweating. Deep breaths. Lights blinding him from the flashes of the camera. Now, this event was broadcast live. Several people were in attendance, and Nik himself said he was nervous yet excited for this opportunity. So, confidently he stepped up onto the platform and began his walk.

Before his venture, what if Nik took a deep breath and turned to the crowd? I'm sure the people would suddenly become silent as Nik turned, wondering what he might say. Facing the audience, he would ask, "Who thinks I can actually do this?" As you can imagine, everyone in attendance,

I'm sure, would raise their hands, fully assured in his preparation. "You can do it, Nik! We believe in you!" fans would shout from afar.

"Okay. Okay," Nik said as he probably tried to relax. "Now, who thinks I can cross Niagara Falls on a tightrope, blindfolded?" Once again, several people among the crowd might put their hands in the air. "We do, Nik! You've been training years for this moment! You got this!" If this reaction were true, I'm sure Nik could tell that the crowd was confident in him to successfully walk the tightrope. He might pause for a moment, look into the crowd once again, and ask one final question. "I have one last question for you all before I begin my walk," he would say. "Who thinks I can carry them on my shoulders while balancing over Niagara Falls?"

The crowd might look surprised by such a question. I know I would. Yet no one in attendance would even dare to raise their hand, wondering what would happen if they did. Maybe the people thought that he would actually go through with it and carry the person who volunteered with him on this adventure.

Now, I have to confess something. Nik didn't actually say any of this. He walked onto the wire confidently and courageously, as the media portrays. I can honestly say that Nik successfully made it across Niagara Falls! Imagine, though, if God were taking this walk instead of Nik. You might be saying, *Sierra, if God can calm the storm in the story of Jonah, no doubt He can cross a tightrope successfully above Niagara Falls.* Understandable, but stay with me. Let's personalize it for a moment.

First question, "Do you think I (God) can make it across this tightrope?"

"Piece of cake," you might say. So, onto the second question:

"Do you think I (God) can make it across blindfolded?"

Feeling no pressure, you might reply, "Of course I do."

Last but not least, "How about with Me (God) carrying you?" Scared of the unknown, you instantly freeze in place, quickly regretting the initial confidence in the first two questions that were asked. Trust is the common denominator.

Personally, I believe that God can do anything and everything He wants with my life. With that being said, that doesn't mean faith comes naturally to me. A lot of times, the things God is calling me to do are scary and are usually out of my comfort zone. Most of the time, I say, "God, you've got this. You can lead my life in whatever direction you want." The reality is, though, I'm fearful and don't trust Him enough to do what He is asking of me. Ever been there? I get so wrapped up in the things I can't do on a human scale (how hard the process might be, people's opinions on the subject, the never-ending line of excuses that play inside my mind). However, I have the Holy Spirit living inside of me! Therefore, I can conquer anything and everything God wants me to do because I am empowered by Him. He has already won this battle by dying on the cross. So what am I afraid of? The battle is already won, so why don't I trust God enough to help me defeat my enemies, fears, and shortcomings?

Has this ever happened to you? You've wanted to do God's will, but when the time comes, you are hesitant in trusting the process. That He *really* has you. He is really for you. He is with you every step of the way. I've been there. It can be challenging to take that leap of faith and trust to do God's calling. I promise that if you do, your confidence and faith in Him will not only grow, but you will become a better you because you took a leap of faith for the Lord.

In the same way, faith by itself, if it is not accompanied by action, is dead. But someone will say, "You have faith; I have deeds." Show me your faith without deeds, and I will show you my faith by my deeds.

—James 2:17–18 (NIV)

Be strong and courageous! Do not be afraid and do not panic before them. For the Lord your God will personally go ahead of you. He will neither fail you nor abandon you.

—Deuteronomy 31:6 (NLT)

At the start of this segment, I added not one but two Bible verses because I thought it was essential. At the beginning of this paragraph, I added two more because it is essential too. Having trust can be difficult, yet it is so vital in our walk with the Lord. Reality is, faith and trust go hand in hand. Believing, like trusting, is making a decision, yet faith is following that decision through action. In order to have faith in someone or something, you need to trust them.

Let me give you another visual. If someone gives you a chair to sit in, would you? I mean, it depends on the look of the chair, am I right? This chair, though, has four sturdy legs. It appears to be in good condition and not wobbly or shaky. You believe the chair will hold you up. Now, let's break here for a moment. Believing can only get you so far. You can believe all day long that the chair will hold you, but until you actually take action and sit in it, you will truly never know. So you act and sit in the chair, confident that it will do the task it was made to do. God is the same way. In order to fully embrace the life God has for you, it involves trust. Your trust, then, involves action through steps of faith and obedience. You have to trust that He will never fail you, never let you down, yet always be there to carry you every step of the way.

Maybe you think God has let you down in some way. You might think He hasn't been there when you needed Him most. You might feel that God has left you hung out to dry. Let me be the first to say that I'm sorry about the things that have happened to you. I'm sorry that you didn't feel loved, appreciated, or even wanted. I'm sorry that you have had to overcome obstacles and challenges that no one ever wants to face. If this is you, your trust may be broken, shattered, and in dire need of restoring. To overcome this obstacle, it takes a lot of prayer and diligence. Mind you, it is never too late to mend that broken relationship. It is never too late to forgive. It is never too late to take the first step in trusting God with your life. Just remember that God has already won the war! Therefore, what should you and I have to fear in trusting Him with our lives?

Do you really trust God with your life and the plans He has for you? How do you know this to be true?

What are some life experiences that have allowed you to solely trust in God's plan?

There Will Be Consequences If You Don't Obey

There are stories all over the Bible about obeying the Lord. The first one that comes to my mind, though, is the story of Adam and Eve. This story is found in Genesis and leads up to all the events that the Bible contains, if you can believe that. Let me tell you about it.

First, let me set the scene. Picture it.

In the beginning, God created the Heavens and the Earth.
—Genesis 1:1 (NLT)

Days of Creation:
- Day 1—Light and darkness were created.
- Day 2—The sky was made.
- Day 3—Land (plants and trees) and water were formed.
- Day 4—The sun, moon, and stars were all created.
- Day 5—Animals that fly and ocean life were made.
- Day 6—Humans were formed in the image of God, and land animals came to be.
- Day 7—God rested.

Leading up to the story of Adam and Eve, God had already been working steadily for five days. Now, after God made everything leading up to humans, the Bible states, "God made _____, and it was good." Basically, no corruption or evil was on the earth. Everything God had made pleased Him. In Genesis 2:7, it states that the Lord formed man from the dust of the ground. He breathed into the man's nostrils, making him alive. After humans were formed, though, He said it was very good because He made them into His own image (Genesis 1:26).

Soon after, God made a garden just east, in Eden, where Adam lived. There, God planted the most beautiful and luscious plants in all the land. In the middle of the garden, He placed two trees. One was called the tree of life and the other was the tree of good and evil. Adam was placed in this garden to watch and tend it. Like I mentioned earlier, God made everything in the garden. Yet He also made things that could be tempting and enticing to the people and animals that lived there if they used it in a negative manner. The Lord then warned Adam, "You can eat from anything in the garden except the tree of good and evil. If you do, you will die." After this, Adam eventually gave names to all of the animals in the garden. When God saw that it was not right for man to be alone, He made a woman, named Eve, who was formed out of Adam's rib.

Okay. Now the scene is set; on with the story.

Chapter three of Genesis is where the disobedience comes into play. You see, Satan (the evil serpent) asked Eve a question. "Did God really say you must not eat from any trees in the garden?" Right then and there, Satan planted a seed of doubt in Eve's mind. The woman responded by telling him what God said to Adam, "We can eat from any fruit or tree in the garden except the tree of good and evil. If we eat it, or even touch it, we will die."

"You won't die," said the serpent. "Instead, you will be like God, knowing both good and evil." Satan was using trickery and lying to Eve. Despite what God had said, Eve now was convinced that the fruit wasn't that bad. So Eve picked the forbidden fruit and gave some to her husband, and both of them ate it. At that moment, both of their eyes were opened. Not just physically, but spiritually. Immediately, they felt shame and guilt for going against the Lord. So much so that they thought they could hide from Him. Mind you, it didn't play out in their favor. Thus, the world had become sinful.

Nothing in all creation is hidden from God. Everything is naked and exposed

before His eyes, and He is the one to whom we are accountable.
—Hebrews 4:13 (NLT)

Now, Adam and Eve both blamed someone for their disobedience to the Lord. Adam blamed Eve, and Eve blamed the serpent. Remember me saying you are responsible for you own sin? It applies here. Remember me saying your sin doesn't just affect you? It also applies here. Basically, when Adam and Eve sinned on that day in the Garden of Eden, that sin caused the whole world to be of a sinful nature. Emotional hardships, physical damages, and spiritual pain are all the result of Adam's and Eve's doing. Since we are sons and daughters of Adam and Eve (the first humans God created), we are all considered sinners and under the penalty of their sin.

Do you have a tendency to blame others for your sinful actions?

Because of this, we sin on a monthly, weekly, and daily basis. If we are born of this earth, we are sinners. As a result, death has entered the world, according to Romans 5:14. Death is a powerful word in these verses. All of us are going to pass away at one time or another, according to Romans 5:15. There is no denying that. Since Adam and Eve both sinned, it led to condemnation throughout the entire world (Romans 5:16). However, one act of righteousness leads to justification for all men. Now, what does this mean without using all of this fancy terminology? Whatever sin (lying, stealing, disobedience, to name a few) you commit, it can be paid in full. God put all of the world's sin on His shoulders when He died on the cross. Therefore, He has forgiven all of our sins (John 1:29). No sin can ever be so big, so foolish, or so scarring that God can't remove it from your life. There is no way to turn the clock back and start over. What's done is done. With that being said, we can only progress and conquer evil by reading scripture, resisting temptation, and trusting God.

He purchased our freedom with the blood of His Son and forgave our sins.
—Ephesians 1:7 (NLT)

But if we confess our sins to Him, He is faithful and just to forgive us our sins and to cleanse us from all wickedness.
—1 John 1:9 (NLT)

[God] has removed our sins as far from us as the east is from the west.
—Psalm 103:12 (NLT)

I want to clarify something. When we turn our life over to Christ and surrender to Him, He takes our sin and washes it clean. No doubt about that. I wholeheartedly believe that He forgives us when we do wrong and go against Him. Yet just because God forgives all of our sin doesn't give us the right to sin more. The whole objective of Christianity is to love God (who is perfect) by living a life that pleases and glorifies Him. On the contrary, sin is something that is imperfect. Since this is the case, believers shouldn't want to keep on sinning and become more imperfect people. That is the opposite of what Christians should aspire to be. When we do sin, knowing it is wrong, are we really saved to begin with? I agree that we will sin more times than we can count, but that doesn't mean we should continue to delve into sin once we have been forgiven of it.

Well then, since God's grace has set us free from the law, does that mean we can go on sinning? Of course not!

—Romans 6:15 (NLT)

The Holy Spirit can call anyone. Usually, the Holy Spirit tugs at a person's heart and wants them to repent or turn from their sin. This is called conviction. God wants you to give your sin to Him so you can be forgiven and not be burdened by it any longer. If you think you don't have any sin in your life, you are only fooling yourself. No one likes to be reminded of their past mistakes, including me. Lucky for us, God isn't a God who brings up the past. He wants to wipe the slate clean and start from scratch. When you have the Holy Spirit in your heart, you should want to strive to do what is right in the eyes of the Lord. After all, Christians look to the One who was made perfect and never sinned. As believers, it is our job to be "little Christs" and continually seek His will for our lives, for He will never steer us in the wrong direction.

My child, don't reject the Lord's discipline; and do not be upset when He corrects you. For the Lord corrects those He loves, just as a father corrects a child in whom he delights.

—Proverbs 3:11–12 (NLT)

As I previously mentioned, because Adam and Eve sinned, this led to the world becoming sinful. Both of them felt shame and knew that they had done wrong in the Lord's sight. There were consequences for their actions. Has that ever happened to you? As an infant or toddler, maybe your parents told you to not touch a hot iron, a sharp knife, or a glass item on the counter. You may have gotten a spanking or a hit on the hand if you came near those things. I have not experienced parenthood yet, but I assume it can be a fine line to cross. On one hand, we don't want our children to get hurt or experience pain, yet we want them to feel safe and protected from the world. As they grow older, though, maybe they need to make their own mistakes because that is how they learn.

As a parent disciplines their children, God also disciplines those He loves. When I first got baptized and surrendered my life to Christ at age eleven, I was like an infant. I had to learn what pleased Him and have discipline in my actions for knowing Him more. Sure, I made a lot of mistakes, but I grew my faith because of it. As I became older and my faith started to mature, I realized what made my relationship with the Lord strong and what could potentially have negative effects on it. When I did make mistakes in my walk (which was often), I would become extremely convicted. Now, conviction is a good thing. It shows that you have the Lord in you and He is urging you back on the right path. However, it is up to you to choose which path to take.

The Bible has mini-stories called parables that basically teach a lesson as you read. Well, in the book of Luke, there are three distinct parables that portray something that is lost but one day is found. They are the Parable of the Lost Sheep (Luke 15:1–7), the Parable of the Lost Coin (vs. 8–10), and the Parable of the Lost Son (vs. 11–32). In the parable about the lost son, a man had two sons. Before their father died, the youngest son wanted his share of his father's estate and to become wealthy. Being the generous father that he was, he divided the money and gave half to his youngest. Shortly after, though, the youngest son moved off and wasted all of the money on wild living. Soon, a great famine swept over the land. Since the son had no money to buy food, he began to starve. He had to find work, so he got hired as a pig farmer to earn money to buy food. Because he was extremely hungry, even the pig's slop looked good to him. It didn't take long for the son to come to his senses and realize that he had made a huge mistake in his lifestyle, one that he thought he couldn't come back from.

"I want to go home!" he cried. The son knew he had done wrong. He felt so ashamed and embarrassed for what he had done. After all, he blew all of his father's savings on a life that wasn't good. So he didn't think he was worthy any longer to be considered a part of the family. Still, he wanted to try to return home to his father and brother. As he was making the trek home, his father saw him coming from a great distance and ran to embrace him. The father didn't walk over to him but ran, arms stretched out and ready to hold his son again. Love and compassion were greatly displayed. Once they came together, the father never questioned his son's actions but instead celebrated his arrival. The details of his actions were unnecessary. All that mattered was that the son returned home to his father. Being that the son was almost forgone, his father still embraced him with open arms, threw a party for him, and gave him the finest meal and clothing imaginable regardless of the life he once lived.

There will be more joy in Heaven over one sinner who repents than over ninety-nine righteous persons who need no repentance.
—Luke 15:7 (ESV)

Just like a good parent, God will always discipline His children. I am sure that it is hard to watch your child make their own mistakes, continually going back to a life that you didn't picture for them. Sometimes, though, the child can rebel and keep running in the opposite direction. Depending on the parent, when their child decides to return, some may fully embrace them and welcome them home with celebration and relief, while others may not be so lucky. When this does happen, remember that no matter how hard, far, or fast you continue to run in the opposite direction, God has never left you. The Parable of the Lost Son resembles God embracing His child when they wonder off. If this sounds like you, God won't ask questions or make you feel guilty about what you did. His only concern is holding you again. God's arms will always be open and ready to receive you as His child. No matter what you have done, how bad you think you've messed up, or how far off course you might seem, when you finally decide enough is enough and turn back to God, He rejoices and celebrates your homecoming ever so abundantly!

If this sounds like you, aren't you tired of running? Tired of trying to find joy and fulfillment in the next best thing? Tired of finding false hope in someone or something that will only let your down? My friend, I encourage you to come to the cross today. Lay your burdens down and let God call you His child once again.

What makes you hesitant to run to God instead of away from Him?

Chapter 6
Spot the Difference

You are the light of the world—like a city on a hilltop that cannot be hidden.
- Matthew 5:14 (NLT)

Whenever my family and I go to a restaurant, my niece and nephew get kiddie menus to look at, along with crayons to solve activity puzzles. Many times they want me to play tic-tac-toe or help them figure out the coolest crossword or unscramble puzzle. Those are all fun games, but I always seem to be drawn to the spot-the-difference activity first. This game is pretty self-explanatory. Basically, the puzzle has two pictures side by side. All you have to do is circle what is different about them.

Now, I like to associate this game with real life. I tend to think... *What is different about me that stand out from the rest of mankind?* Many things can be considered different in this case. Some people may play sports, and maybe you're not the athletic type. Others may be very creative, while you are lucky just to draw a stick figure. God made each of us with special talents and abilities. However, what I am talking about in this chapter is something that makes believers stand out from nonbelievers. If someone went up to you and asked if you are a Christian, that should really offend you. No one should have to ask if you are a believer or not. Rather, your life should be a testimony of who you live for. It should show evidence that you are a child of God by the way you speak, serve others, and exude joy, peace, and confidence even in the midst of trials and hardships.

So, how is that going for you? If you say you are a believer, are others seeing Him through what you project? Is the Lord affecting your attitude, speech, and self-worth? If so, how? I admit that choosing these actions doesn't make us believers, but they actively show that we live a life for Jesus.

If you are having trouble with showing kindness to your enemies, using positive and encouraging words, or displaying confidence, you are not alone. I have trouble with them to this day too. However, when writing this book, I prayed that both of us would get insight on how to navigate these bumpy obstacles with a few of these tips and challenges.

Kill 'Em with Kindness

But the Lord said to Samuel, "Don't judge by his appearance or height, for I have rejected him. The Lord doesn't see things the way you see them. People judge by outward appearance, but the Lord looks at the heart."
—1 Samuel 16:7 (NLT)

It was a regular day in a small Baptist church in Tennessee. All the women were dressed to the nines in fancy dresses along with their hats and pearls, while the men looked dashing in their blue suits and khaki pants. The sun beamed through the stained-glass window welcoming the congregation in. As they normally did, Mrs. Penny and Mr. Jacobs stood in the foyer greeting the people who came into the church that morning.

Like most Sundays, before the church service began, the congregation had fellowship with one another. You could hear "It is so good to see you; my, don't you look nice today; how has your week been? Are the wife and kids doing all right?" as people passed by each other being welcomed with a friendly hug, a handshake, a smile, or a quick chat. Suddenly, a gentleman approached the pulpit. "Pastor Peter isn't going to be with us for a couple of weeks. He went on a trip with his wife." As the congregation quickly took their seats, they looked surprised but also relieved, knowing that the pastor and his wife were getting some time to themselves. At that time, the guest speaker made his way to the stage.

Once the speaker began preaching, a middle-aged man came into the church quickly and quietly and found an open seat in the very back row. His clothes looked tattered and worn, his face was scarred, the stench on his clothes was enough to make you gag, and his hands and hair seemed to be all knotted and rather dirty, as if he needed a long shower. Everyone that was around him, especially kids, gave him glares and rude whispers as if to say, "What is he doing here?" As the speaker finished his sermon, the congregation prayed and was dismissed. When everyone was leaving, they all gave goodbye hugs to one another as they talked their way out the door. Once the majority of the people had dispersed, the man who sat in the back row slowly walked out without so much as a warm welcome or a friendly goodbye.

Another week passed, and it was Sunday again. The routine was still the same: hugs, handshakes, and a friendly smile upon entering. As the congregation took their seats to begin the sermon, a woman came in dressed in her finest clothes. She wore a blue lace dress with ruffles on the collar, three-inch heels, and diamonds on her ears, with a gold necklace to match.

Many people were welcoming her as she found a seat in the back row. Once the message had ended, the woman quickly was bombarded with people around her. "Let me introduce myself," they would say. One by one people approached this woman as if she were a celebrity. Soon, her feet quickly became tired, and she made her way toward the door. "Come back and see us," Mrs. Penny said as she opened the door to let her out.

After a couple of weeks, Pastor Peter was back. He shook hands with the people in the congregation and gave friendly smiles to people from afar who were in attendance. He got up in the pulpit and waited for the crowd to become silent. "Today," he started, "I am glad to be back." He took a sip of water, gazed around the room, and then continued. "I am glad to be back, but I am highly disappointed." Smiles quickly faded as the congregation could tell that something was off. "Deacon Mitchel said I would be gone for a couple of weeks with my wife, and he was right. Many of you probably wanted to know where we went. We didn't go on vacation to another state or go on a cruise overseas. Instead, we were here." Confused about what he meant, the room got so quiet you could hear a pin drop. "Some of you may remember a middle-aged man who came into church a couple of weeks ago. He sat in the back row and wore a brown shirt that was faded and blue jeans that were ripped and dirty. He also had on boots that were torn at the bottom. It was brought to my attention that no one welcomed this man at all, not even so much as a smile, while entering or exiting the church."

As he spoke, the majority of the people sat silent in disbelief. They were a bit surprised to hear these words on a Sunday morning, let alone from a pastor that wasn't even in church to witness it.

The pastor continued, "Last week, a lady visited here and was welcomed with open arms. She wore nice clothes, and it seemed like everyone made her feel welcome." Suddenly, one gentleman who was becoming more and more agitated piped up and asked, "By chance, if this is true, preacher, if you and your wife were gone, how do you know all this?"

"Oh, but I wasn't gone," said the preacher. "I was in church the whole time. I wasn't wearing what I usually do on a Sunday morning, though. You see," said Pastor Peter, "I got some worn-out clothes from a thrift store, had someone do my makeup and hair, and disguised myself as a man off the streets. I pretended to be that middle-aged man who came in two Sundays ago while my cousin from out of town, whom you've never met, was the lady who visited last week. Some of you may think this was a dirty trick, but I wanted to see how the congregation acted when I wasn't around. And now I know," he said, with a disappointed look. Everyone in attendance was shocked at the pastor's words. Overcome with disappointment, Pastor Peter took a few moments to let this sink in and then began to preach. "Today's message," said the pastor, "is about kindness."

Words

Words Have Meaning

Did you know over three hundred thousand words are in the dictionary? Mind-blowing, isn't it? My family plays Scrabble quite often, so using the dictionary comes in handy, along with the infamous Google. It also helps that each word is alphabetized and defines the word and its part of speech. Despite the length, each word in the dictionary has at least one definition italicized right beside it, while others might have more. For example, the word *set* in the Oxford dictionary has several definitions, while the word *yogurt* has only one. Even though the dictionary has numerous pages with thousands of words, every year people decide to come up with new and interesting words to add to the list.

Depending on their mood, people use words hundreds of times a day. We converse at work, in school, and at the doctor's office. People socialize over celebrations like Christmas, Thanksgiving, birthdays, or graduations. Others communicate while doing chores around the house, talking on the phone, or texting with one another. Whatever the case, people talk to each other daily. But have you thought about the words that you actually say to others around you? Have you noticed the tone in which you speak, the rate at which you speak, and the body language you use when you speak? To be honest, until writing this section, I haven't thought much about it up until now. I've come to realize, though, that the words you say have a significant impact on a person's life.

Have you ever texted someone and the person on the receiving end thought it came across another way? I've been on the receiving end of messages, and I honestly had to question their intention behind it for me to respond. Like, "Did they really mean it this way?" One thing about text messaging, you can't see the other person's body language or hear their tone of voice. In a conversation face-to-face, I'm sure you can tell if a person is happy, upset, disappointed, or angry just by their facial expression. If they begin talking, their voice can be high if they're excited, direct when angry or upset, or sad because they are disappointed. Many things can contribute to having a clear conversation via face-to-face. Not so clear via text messaging. Now, I'm not bashing texting at all. It is a good way to communicate at an individual's pace. However, it is not the greatest when trying to have a conversation that may or may not be important.

I remember a kid in high school who was on the football team. His name was Brad. This guy was one of the best on the team and was always looked up to by his younger peers. This season the team was up against one of the best in the district. To prepare for the game, every day Brad would lead his team in warm-ups while practicing after school. Many teachers would encourage him throughout the week and give him compliments on his athleticism while he was in their classes. His family even would help him with chores around the house to ensure that he wasn't too tired to give 100 percent in the classroom and on the field. You could say that Brad was very determined, driven, and dedicated in all of his successes. It seems like every person was counting on him to come home with a win. All except the one who really mattered to him, Mina, his girlfriend.

You see, Mina was the type of person that all eyes had to be on her. Nothing was ever good enough to suit her. All the boys swooned over her because of how beautiful and popular she was, yet she was a jerk to everyone she knew. She was too prissy for my liking. I guess it was obvious why Brad and Mina were together. All the guys wanted her, including Brad, and she wanted a quarterback guy. Brad fit that mold just right.

Game day finally arrived. Brad's nerves were intensifying as game time got closer. The morning of the game, Mina decided to pay a visit to Brad's house so they could talk. They went outside and sat on the swing. "You better win today, Brad," Mina said in a strong tone. "If you don't, you can forget about us."

"All because of a game?" he asked.

"Well, now that you mention it," she said, "There is more to the story. In math class, you never look at me when I make eye contact with you. You seem to always want to hang around with your friends rather than go shopping with me, and you never give me compliments in front of our friends anymore. You're so egotistical! Just remember, no win, no us."

You could tell that this shook Brad to his core. Yet before he even had a chance to respond, Mina got in her car and drove off in her shiny red convertible.

It was time for the big game. The stands were packed as fans started to cheer when the team came through the end zone and onto the field. The team not only was energized but also felt confident, knowing that their team would win.

"How do you feel today, Brad?" his coach asked.

"Not too good," Brad responded.

"Shake it off," the coach told him. "We've got a game to win."

Brad had forgotten all of the compliments his peers and teachers gave him throughout the week. That was all washed away, thanks to Mina. He lost his focus. Nothing mattered more to Brad than to win the game. Not because he wanted to win. Not because his teachers, coaches, and school were all counting on him, but because of his girlfriend.

The game was underway, and Brad made fumble after fumble. Pass interception after pass interception. You could clearly tell he wasn't in the right headspace to lead this team. He wasn't happy playing the game he loved, all because he felt pressure from his girlfriend. He couldn't shake her words, "You're so egotistical," out of his head, which made him play worse than usual. The coach at that time didn't have another quarterback, so Brad was their only chance. As you can imagine, because Brad wasn't himself, they lost the game. Yes, Brad lost some friends in due time, but most importantly, he lost the one thing he thought he couldn't live without, his precious Mina.

Years went by and Brad got scholarships to play professional college football. As always, the women were all after him because of his strength, personality, and intelligence. While he got many compliments and praises over the years, he never could quite forget what Mina said to him all those years ago. The words would replay in his head every now and again, but that saying didn't deter Brad from succeeding to the fullest!

Words are like a tube of toothpaste. Once emptied, you can't put all the toothpaste back in the tube no matter how hard you try. After you say them, there is no taking them back. I wholeheartedly think that you can forgive the words being said to you but not necessarily forget them. They are out in the open. Ephesians 4:29 states that we should let no unwholesome word come out of our mouth. Meaning, we need to speak with kindness and encouragement, not mockery or hatred. The words you speak can either build a person up or tear them down. So be mindful of the things you say. Your words have meaning. Your words do matter. You never know how it can affect others around you. You make the choice of how to use them.

Are the words you choose reflecting Christ?

Words Are Powerful

These people honor me with their lips, but their hearts are far from me.
—Matthew 15:8 (NLT)

I just mentioned that the words you speak have meaning. Now, let's talk about their power. Words are powerful, just like actions. Your actions, as well as your words, say a lot about you as an individual. I wrote about actions in a previous chapter; now let's talk about words and how they can be either uplifting or damaging to yourself and others around you.

As stated already, words have significant power and shouldn't be used lightly. Sometimes, I forget how impactful words can be. I mean, ever heard the saying "Sticks and stones may break my bones, but words may never hurt me?" Yeah...not true. That is definitely a lie. Words do hurt. I'm not going to say that they don't. With that being said, when we know the power behind the words that we say, hopefully we will approach situations with more grace and patience, knowing that how we use them will greatly affect those in our circle of influence.

First off, words have the power to influence us, whether positively or negatively. I experienced this firsthand. When I was a teenager, my friends were partaking in activities that I didn't care to do. One of those things involved drinking. This was something that I didn't care to indulge in, but my friends thought otherwise. "Do it just this once. Quit being a stick-in-the-mud. You know you want to," they would say. Truthfully, I didn't care what they thought. It was my life, and I wasn't going to do something that I didn't want to do. Yet their words did sting. Although I said I didn't care, going home that night, I replayed the conversation in my head. *Should I have drunk like the other girls? Did they really see me as boring?* They could have influenced me to go in a direction I didn't want to go, but I didn't let them. I knew where I stood and wouldn't budge. When I told my mom what happened that night, she was proud I stood my ground. Although she was surprised that the incident occurred, her words were very optimistic and positive. Ever since then, I have learned to speak inspiring words to others as well as myself, knowing that it will make a significant difference in our lives.

Who do you think you are influencing by the words that you speak?

Authoritativeness is another way words have power. Speaking with boldness says a lot about what you say. I wholeheartedly think that speaking in Jesus's name has the greatest authority over anything this world says. I'm ashamed to say I've always thought this way but never really put it into practice until I was faced with depression and anxiety. During that time, I did it ritually. Let me be real. I would lie awake at night almost frozen in my bed, sobbing and pleading with God to get me out of that dark and lonely pit. Usually when that happened, I ended up getting very little sleep. Whenever I would wake up in the middle of the night, which was often, I would quote scripture out loud. I wouldn't say it in my head, but I would speak it into existence. I would quote it in first-person rather than second-person. Whenever there is a you in the verse, I would replace that word with me or I. One of the main verses was 1 Corinthians 10:13. Specifically, I would pray these words...

"No temptation has overtaken you (me) except such as is common to man. But God is faithful; He will not allow you (me) to be tempted beyond what you (I) are (am) able. But with the temptation, He will also make the way of escape, so that you (I) may be able to bear it (NKJV)...In Jesus's name, Amen."

I couldn't tell you the number of times I spoke these words over myself, not timidly or nervously, but confidently, knowing that God had me during that time. I wouldn't just speak it into existence, but I would speak it into existence with authority. My belief in God was stronger than my battle. I knew that as a believer, God would take care of me, and that the battle would pass. I've come to realize that a person's strength is not defined by who they are but rather what they have at their disposal. As a Christian, this means that God and His unwavering power had to be my strength in this time of trial. Because of this, I didn't just want to keep that power in my head. I wanted the enemy to know God had authority over my life. So I spoke my prayers out loud, letting the enemy recognize that I wasn't scared of the flaming arrows being thrown at me. Although I didn't know how long the storm would last, I was confident, knowing that the words I was speaking were with God's authority and not my own. Speaking in Jesus's name shows the enemy that he has no control over you. It is one thing to speak it, but you actually have to believe it. Do you truly believe that He can get you through any trial you may face in Jesus's name? In Jesus's name, do you believe He has the power to help you, to hold you, to strengthen you, to protect you? Don't let words have authority over you, but allow God's word to direct and guide you. I can confidently say that Jesus has the power to work miracles in your life. Believe and let Him in. The hymn is so true... there is something about that name!

You made all the delicate, inner parts in my body and knit me together in my mother's womb. Thank you for making me so wonderfully complex.
—Psalm 139:13–14 (NLT)

Many members of my family put this into action when I was born. My mom went into what she thought was going to be a normal sonogram appointment, but instead she came out in an ambulance being rushed to the hospital. The doctors told her that she had to stay on bed rest until she had me because she had severe preeclampsia. Mind you, this was early November, and I wasn't supposed to be born until late March. So having to hear that she would have to stay in the hospital for four months was indeed a shock! I'm sure my mom was very confused and extremely anxious not knowing the outcome of her health and my own. Honestly, the doctors and nurses didn't think I had much of a chance. After weeks in the hospital and a strenuous C-section later, I came out weighing a little over one pound. Nevertheless, the doctors said I was beet-red and had a good set of pipes. "She's a fighter," they said. However, I was not in the clear and had a long road ahead.

Being that I was three months premature, my eyes had not fully developed, and my heart and lungs needed some intensive TLC, so they immediately rushed me to the NICU where the premature babies were kept. After a grueling and prayerful four months of being in the NICU, I was finally able to come home. Needless to say, the story of my birth definitely made my family seek God more and pray harder than ever. Yes, they prayed for me to ultimately live and grow up to be happy and healthy, but they were terrified that the outcome would be different than they had planned. Regardless of the circumstance and hardship they were facing, my family was hopeful and prayed with the utmost authority to God, knowing He would do as He saw fit.

Obviously you know what happened next. The Lord indeed answered my family's prayers. Though the Lord saw fit to save my mom's life and give me an opportunity to live, I think that it is important to consider that not everything you pray for will come to fruition the way you plan. My mom had no idea what she was going to encounter, being rushed to the hospital that day, but she knew who was in control. So she fervently prayed with authority and told God, "If you let my baby live, I will raise her up in church, and she will come to know you." She has been faithful to that promise ever since.

God can give one of three answers to your prayers, either yes, no, or not right now. Despite having prayed that depression and anxiety would cease in my life, I still battle with them to this day. This doesn't mean that God doesn't care about me, but He will use my suffering to bring Him honor and glory in the end. This may be a harsh reality, but God is going to do what He wants to do. He is the Creator of your life and knows everything you do before it even happens. Crazy, right? Even though you pray for a specific thing to happen, God may think differently. When this does happen, it doesn't mean you stop praying altogether. Just because your prayers didn't get answered in the way you want doesn't mean that God doesn't love or value you. He just has a bigger and better plan in mind than you have for yourself. In the verse mentioned above, it states that we were a thought in God's mind of value and purpose. The intricate details of your life, He sees. The thoughts you think, He hears. The unforeseen future, He knows. When people go through hard times, it may feel as though God doesn't see us. I can attest to the fact that the battles that we face are to make us stronger, wiser, and help point others to the Lord. I was able to share about my anxiety and depression with so many girls at camp. After their week was over, they wrote me notes telling me how encouraged they were that I openly shared a challenging piece of my story. Now, I am confidently sharing this battle with you too. Although I still wrestle with these things, I am at peace knowing that my God has me in the midst of a trying time.

What are some instances where you have prayed with authority to God?

How do you feel when you don't get your prayers answered?

Can you look back and see that your unanswered prayers were a blessing in disguise? Explain.

Mirroring the Heart

Guard your heart above all else, for it determines the course of your life.
—Proverbs 4:23 (NLT)

Whenever you look in the mirror, your image stares back at you. That is only the outward appearance. Inward appearance is where your spiritual emotions and desires dwell. I am a person who wears her heart on her sleeve. Everyone I encounter can tell when my mood is off because my face, tone of voice, and body language say it all. Maybe you're a person who doesn't like to show their emotions. Even if you don't show it right then, the little signs of your heart will come to the surface in time. So if people could take a look at your heart right now, what would the message say? Is your heart damaged, in need of mending, or struggling to move? Does it feel weak, exhausted, or heavy? Just like people desire an outward change, you might also be in need of an inward renewal yourself.

The heart is mentioned almost one thousand times throughout the Bible. The Lord speaks about guarding your heart (Proverbs 4:23) and keeping it pure (Psalm 119:9), how deceitful it can be and how it can lead you astray (Jeremiah 17:9), and how your outward actions and attitude reflect your internal spiritual problems (Proverbs 27:19). The words you speak are also a reflection of it. As stated in Proverbs, everything you do flows from your heart and shows the world where your heart is.

The heart is the central part of all humans on this earth. It is the innermost part of one's body. If a person's heart is either bad or damaged in some way, the body tends to shut down, causing muscles and organs not to function properly. This could cause one's life to be in serious jeopardy. With that being said, our heart is in need of the utmost care and attention. Because of this, we are to nurture it and keep it pure in the way we live out our lives.

Our hearts are the vessel in which the mouth speaks. For example, if rage and anger is inside our heart, it will come out in the way we talk to people. Most of the time, the people closest to me get the brunt of my anger and madness. I tend to explode on them, and they weren't even the problem to begin with! Talk about needing a heart change. My anger is reflective of my angry and damaged heart. Or when I am bogged down and stressed, once again my heart is not where it needs to be. It shows in the way I speak to others and in my overall negative, complaining attitude. Everyone is in need of a heart change every now and again. Let's face it: without one a spiritual transformation cannot take place. God wants to get rid of your old, beaten down, tattered heart and change you both inwardly and outwardly. Once I strengthen and nourish my heart with the power that comes from God and His Word, then and only then will He mold and create a new heart within me, one that lives for Him. He can do the same thing for you too!

It isn't just a onetime occurrence, though. Because of my sin and conviction, God changes my heart daily. Once a person has made this change, it is easy to get into the one-and-done mentality. *I don't need to repent and turn to the Lord. I've come this far with it being damaged and frayed.*

Why start now? My response is: Why not start now?! I want to encourage you that no matter how shattered your heart may be, God is the ultimate surgeon. He has the ability to give you a fresh and pure heart by removing your old one. No longer is that prevalent in your life. By having a heart change, I pray that my heart will hopefully reflect God's heart in the way I serve, speak to others, and love people well. Being humble, showing kindness, and loving others are all reflections of God and what He did for others while He was on the earth. If we let God renew our hearts daily by reading His Word and praying, we will see things from His perspective and become more positive, kind, patient, and generous to one another while also having a Christ-like attitude. So, examine yourself. Don't be weighed down by your heavy and burdened heart. Instead, I pray that you receive God's heart today and let it transform you from the inside out.

Do you need God to transform your heart?

How can you have a heart that is like God?

The Sound of Silence (Thoughts)

Not only can words be powerful and have a significant effect on us, but our thought process can too. What you think about on a daily basis can affect so many things. It can control how you act toward people and whether you partake in activities or not. Your thoughts have a say in your overall decisions. So, how is your thought life? Are you constantly putting yourself down? Saying a rude comment in your head about another person? Thinking things that you might be ashamed to say out loud? The mind is a powerful thing. Just like anything, it is a process. Our thoughts eventually become actions. Those actions often turn into habits that can snowball into a life that you weren't made to live. No one wants that. It all starts with one small thought. So I encourage you to think upon things that correspond with God's Word.

Do not be conformed to this world, but be transformed by the renewal of your mind, that by testing you may discern what is the will of God, what is good and acceptable and perfect.

—Romans 12:2 (ESV)

In order to achieve this, I am going to share two words that are crucial for our thought life: transform and renewal. These two words have a life-changing impact on the way we view life, ourselves, and others around us. In the book of Ephesians, chapter five, God calls us to put on the helmet of salvation. Although the Lord wants us to put on the whole armor of God (the belt of truth, the breastplate of righteousness, the gospel of peace, the shield of faith, and the sword of the Spirit), the helmet correlates with our thought process. In order to think upon good things, we need to keep our thoughts focused on Godly things, plain and simple.

Ever looked in the mirror and noticed things about yourself that you don't like? Maybe your weight isn't where you want it to be. You might be fixated on you freckles, braces, and glasses. Don't even get me started on the ears and eyebrows! Throughout the day you start to think negatively about yourself. *If I were skinny like her, I'd have a boyfriend. These glasses and braces make me look like a dweeb.* In order to change those appearances, you start going to the gym and eating right to obtain a better physique. You go to your eye doctor and dentist and ask if something could be done to get contacts and Invisalign, all because you didn't like what you saw in the mirror the day before. Now, let me be frank. I am all for changes and wanting people to become better. What I don't like is people changing themselves for the wrong reason. In this case: getting someone to notice you. However, did you see that it all started with a thought? One simple thought can lead to positive or negative actions. Those actions, then, can lead to habits that can make or break you as a person.

What about this? You're sitting alone at the lunch table. Your friend has gone a different direction and started sitting with the popular crowd. Now, you don't want to draw attention to yourself by getting up and moving to join them, so you just sit there. No one is sitting near you, so you continually stare at your plate of corndogs and fries, alone with your thoughts. Sitting in silence, you begin to think, *Why doesn't she want to sit by me? Did I do something wrong? Did I do something to make her mad? Am I the problem?* Or your thoughts can lead you in another direction. *Look at her over there. She thinks she is so popular with her designer clothes and makeup. Well, she can forget about being my friend if she wants to go and sit with the "populars" and leave me hanging. Now that I think about it, she has been acting fake and judgmental lately. Not only that, she didn't even want to study with me for the test on Friday, like we do every week. Who needs her?*

That might be an overexaggerated example, but can you see how your thoughts can sometimes overshadow your true feelings about a person? Sometimes, thinking about others in a negative way can cause you to become bitter toward them. Then the bitterness that is welling up inside can be followed by hatred, something that isn't in God's vocabulary. Don't hate or think negatively about yourself or another person. God wants us to live in harmony with one another.

Here is one more. Suppose your roommate or sibling was out of the house for the night. So you have the whole house—the whole room—to yourself! It's so nice to have alone time once in a while, am I right? You do all the things you normally wouldn't do when another person was there. Blare loud music, don't clean or pick up after yourself, and sing way off-key. Some people tend to go all out when they are alone for a night. Nevertheless, you begin to get tired, so you hop into bed. As you lay your head on your pillow, your mind begins to wander. Once again you're alone with no one to talk to, only you and your thoughts. So you tend to think about your friend at school that gave you the cold shoulder, your coworker who was rude when you got your cup of coffee, or the grouchy neighbor that cut you off in traffic. Perhaps it's deeper than just surface level. You might think you're the only one going through a certain situation. Maybe you think there is no way out because you can't see the light at the end of the tunnel. Now, some may think I am overplaying this. However, I am an overthinker. Call it a curse. Call it a gift. Whichever and whatever it is, I still need to take precautions about how I think and what goes into my mind. The harsh and true reality is that we live in a world that is negative. TV, social media, songs, and even books can play a big part in our thought process. Are the books I am reading giving into my temptation? Would my parents or kids want to watch the same show I'm watching? Does this song go against my beliefs or use language that I don't agree with? Face it, whatever you see, hear, or experience during the day can pop up in your mind when you least expect it. Therefore, take the necessary precautions to safeguard your mind from the enemy.

Finally, brothers and sisters, whatever is true, whatever is noble, whatever is right, whatever is pure, whatever is lovely, whatever is admirable—if anything is excellent or praiseworthy—think about such things.
—Philippians 4:8 (NIV)

Transforming your mind can be one of the best things you can do to impact your life and other lives for the better. The enemy wants you to get caught up in the problems of today. He wants us to have thoughts that are displeasing to the Lord. He wants us to go against ourselves and talk or think badly about a neighbor or, sometimes, ourself. Christ, though, wants the complete opposite. So, how do we transform our minds? By changing our horizontal focus on the world to a vertical focus on God. Once you begin to stop thinking about the negativity and destruction this world has to offer and get fixated on the positivity and goodness of God, only then will you be able to fully guard and protect your thoughts from spiraling out of control.

Describe your thought life.

What are some things you can do to transform your mind?

Can you think of anything that might cause harmful thoughts (i.e., books, people, TV, music)?

What do you need to get rid of or do differently in order to transform your mind for the better?

The second word is renewal. Putting off our old ways and turning to new ways helps our thought process. New Year's resolutions are a great example of this. It's something that I love to partake in while having goals to aim for. Doing something new, adventurous, and spiritually growing in the upcoming new year is usually at the top of my list. Dieting, saving money, or going on trips might be part of your resolutions as the old year fades. However, do you actually stick with all of them that you set for yourself? Some might, but most of the time, within a couple weeks, you're back where you started. You don't have to wait for a new year to become a better you, just like you don't have to wait a week, a month, or even a year to renew your mindset. Start now, one day at a time. The Apostle Paul tells us not to let our minds be transformed by the world but by the Word. Renewal and change take dedication and discipline to make happen. It is a daily task that requires work and commitment. We are truly renewed when we read and internalize the truths that we find in God's Word. Studying the Bible every day, especially in the morning, gets my mind and heart started in the right direction. It allows my thoughts to be honed in on God and not focused elsewhere. Your mind cannot think of two thoughts at the same time. Therefore, feed it with scripture memorization. That way, when ungodly thoughts do arise (which they will), you will be more apt to face them head-on with the greatest tactic there is: scripture.

What is the first step you can take to renew your mind?

What goal do you have for yourself this week, this month, or this year?

How will having a renewed mindset help you accomplish these goals?

Dodging the Enemy (Confidence)

Be sober-minded; be watchful. Your adversary the devil prowls around like a roaring lion seeking someone to devour.

—1 Peter 5:8 (ESV)

Imagine you and the enemy playing dodgeball. You have a ball in one hand and are ready to throw at the enemy to knock him down. Yet before you do, he picks up a ball and throws it in your direction, hoping to knock you out of the game, which is his goal. However, instead of dodging his throws, you pick up a ball on your side and start blocking all of his shots. As you start to block his throws, you begin to feel more confident as you step closer to the boundary line. Suddenly, the enemy hurls a ball at you, the fastest one yet! Once again, instead of dodging or running scared, you take full advantage and catch his ball before it can knock you down, getting him out of the game. You used strategy to help you win.

I like this example because it does give you a visual aid. The enemy will try to knock you down by any means necessary. Although dodging balls can have its advantages to an extent, it is very different than blocking them. Just picture it. The more he throws, the more you dodge. As you begin to duck and weave to miss his shots, you begin to feel tired and weak. He can see that you are getting fatigued, so he starts throwing the balls faster and harder, making it tougher for you to dodge and ultimately win. Since you are so tired, you start to trip and stumble, leaving him more opportunity to succeed. Now, dodging the enemy's throws will only allow him to try harder to get you out of the game. Don't give him that advantage. God gave you tactics, so use them.

Blocking the enemy means you meet him at the boundary line with a ball in hand, fully confident and ready to win. When he throws a ball, you block his shot. You don't run scared or hide (you can't really hide in dodgeball), but you meet him head-on. He can see that you are ready and willing to do whatever it takes to win. You are saying to the enemy, "You have no power here. I'm going to win this battle whether you like it or not."

So, how do you do it? You use scripture in order to block the enemy's shots. If you begin to dodge his balls rather than block, you will begin to get weaker, and the enemy will become stronger. When he fires those lies at you, you have to push back and block that ball with scripture memorization. Don't allow him to win the battle. Anxiety, depression, lies, stress, anger, jealousy, and comparison are all tactic balls that the enemy can hurl in your direction. If he does, block his shot. Meet him at the boundary line, ready to fight with confidence. God has given you strategies and smarts to overcome anything and everything the enemy tries to throw your way. Don't just dodge the enemy's shots, but block them, knowing that the Lord is on your side, fighting with you through it all.

What scripture references can you use to block the enemy's shots in your own life?

Do you think you can block his shots just by reading scripture? Explain.

Confidently Patient

Has God ever told you to do something, and your first thought was *God, this doesn't make sense?* It can be said that I have questioned God a time or two throughout my own life. When I didn't get a specific job that I worked so hard to achieve, a relationship that ended so abruptly that left my heart shattered, or a tragedy that suddenly occurred, I began to question the Lord during those hard seasons. How about if God didn't answer your prayer right away or give you what you prayed for? To be honest, I would be like… *Remember me? When is it my time, God? When is it my turn? I'm right here, waiting for you to make your move.* Mind you, because of these instances, it can be easy to question God and His plan. I know I have many times. Regardless of the outcome, though, He has a mighty plan for us even if we don't understand the situation firsthand.

A man named Noah sought the Lord in the midst of an unknown situation too. You may have heard the story of Noah and the Ark, but if not, here is a little summary. In the book of Genesis, the Lord saw that the people were increasing in their wickedness. During this time, people sought only to live for themselves while letting their hearts become very evil and violent. They didn't fear the Lord or obey Him anymore but instead wanted to live lives that were reckless and selfish, aiming to please only themselves. Since many people were turning away from the Lord rather than toward Him, He became very angry and displeased. So God conducted a plan to wipe out the corruption of the earth and start from scratch. Noah was a crucial part of that plan becoming a reality.

Look! I am about to cover the earth with a flood that will destroy every living thing that breathes. Everything on earth will die.

—Genesis 6:17 (NLT)

Since Noah was a righteous man from the beginning, God put his faith to the test. God instructed Noah to build a boat called an ark. Because the earth was so massively wicked, God wanted to wipe out the earth completely by flooding it for forty days and forty nights. The ark was to become a flotation device for Noah, his three sons, their wives, and two of every kind of animal during this season. Along with building this gigantic ark, God gave Noah specific instructions to follow. According to Genesis, Noah was six hundred years old when this event even took place!

Build a large boat from cypress wood and waterproof it with tar, inside and out. Then construct decks and stalls throughout its interior. Make the boat 450 feet long, 75 feet wide, and 45 feet high. Leave an 18-inch opening below the roof all the way around the boat. Put the door on the side; and build three decks inside the boat—lower, middle and upper.

—Genesis 6:14–16 (NLT)

Talk about a huge undertaking! I am sure that God wanting to start over was very out of the ordinary in those days. Being that this was a huge task to complete, I'm sure that Noah's family, along with the neighboring community, was all very skeptical about all of this. Nothing like this had ever happened before. Even though things might have been a bit obscure, though, Noah had the utmost confidence in God that His plan would succeed even in the midst of confusion and disbelief from others.

Let me stop here for a moment. People might ask why you are doing certain things for God. They may be a little confused as to why you are spending your time, money, and energy devoted to something that might not come to fruition. However, they don't know your God like you do. Don't let their opinions stop you from aiming to please Him and do what He commands. If Noah only focused on other people's opinions rather than God's command, I'm sure we wouldn't be here today. Your relationship with God is between you and Him. If He calls you to do something, don't listen to the haters and their negative opinions. Keep your energy and mind focused on God and His plan for your life. That's the overall success story.

Are you letting people's opinions dictate what you do for God?

How do you battle against that?

Noah followed the Lord's directions precisely. Two by two the animals boarded the giant ark. Could you imagine the smell that overtook the ark? The noise when Noah and his family were trying to sleep? The hectic living conditions where he and his family ate, slept, and washed? Since they were in tight quarters, this probably involved conflict between his family too. Impatience, I'm sure, started to creep in also. Despite all the chaos, though, Noah was still confident in God's plan even in the center of the hardship and strife.

Noah found favor in the eyes of the Lord among all the confusion that might have occurred. After the flood was over, God sent a rainbow to show that He will never flood the earth again. Even though challenges came with living on the ark, Noah had full assurance that God knew best.

Can you say that about God? When you run into bumps along the way, how do you overcome them? See, Noah was a devoted Christian from the beginning. He wanted to please God even if it didn't make sense to him at the time. Despite his age, Noah overcame tremendous obstacles by building the ark and caring for his family and animals while on the ark for forty days and nights, all while maintaining trust in God that His plan will succeed. If God is calling you to something, though, He has a bigger and better plan than you have for yourself. Like I have mentioned before, the Lord has given you power to do His will regardless of what others think of you or what you think about yourself. I promise, once you strive to please the Lord, His plans (which will become your plans) will come to fruition.

Are you allowing yourself to trust God even in the unknown?

What are some obstacles that might keep you from trusting God?

Are you confident in who God created you to be? If so, how are you acting upon it in your own life?

Chapter 7
The Struggle Is Real

But those who trust in the Lord will find new strength. They will soar high on wings like eagles. They will run and not grow weary. They will walk and not faint.

– Isaiah 40:31 (NLT)

My parents raised me to be a hard worker, have a never-give-up attitude, and not to slack in my efforts to succeed. If you are like me, I tried many things before I found my niche as a preteen. I took horseback-riding lessons, played piano, and even tried my hand at ballet. Nothing stuck until my mom signed me up to march in the band starting in eighth grade. Although I was very apprehensive, I took a shot at the clarinet and was hooked on both marching and playing throughout my middle and high school career.

I knew that playing an instrument could be difficult, but I never assumed that marching while playing an instrument could be even more challenging. Marching in the band was not as easy as some people may think. My band director had us practice two hours every Monday, Tuesday, and Thursday after school near the football field. Now, during most practices it was extremely hot. Some of my friends put on sunscreen and wore hats to shade themselves from the blazing sun. Most of us had to carry what was called a camel pack full of water on our backs and sipped it as we marched without an instrument. There were many times when I came home both tired and hungry, drenched in pure sweat. "Did you drink enough water today?" my mom would ask as I got in the car after practice. I would always reply with an eye roll and a "yes, Mom."

Now, during my first band camp (a summer session where previous band members teach new ones how to march), I fainted on the practice field. Since I had never been to band camp before and was around numerous high schoolers (I was in middle school at the time), it was extremely embarrassing. Did I mention I fainted in front of the entire band, which was about seventy-five members? Yeah...it was totally humiliating! I remember standing in one place while my director was giving instructions, and then suddenly I lay flat on the ground like a pancake. When I came to, my friends were all looking down at me. Not laughing, as I expected, but looking concerned. They helped me up, and I walked inside, where the nurse on duty made sure everything was okay. I informed him that I had been drinking plenty of fluids and seemed to be hydrated.

If you have never fainted before, it is a weird feeling. Your head feels as light as a feather while also leaving you feeling very disoriented at the same time. "Do you remember locking your knees while standing up straight?" the nurse asked. I didn't recall doing anything like that. I had never taken this into consideration, that it could cause fainting and lightheadedness. The nurse then gave me more water and discussed how locking my knees had to do with me being humiliated as I fainted on the practice field. After that day, I tried to drink plenty of water and relax my joints while marching.

You might be asking, *What does fainting have to do with God?* That's a valid question, one that made me think and do a lot of soul-searching myself to find the answer. Here is what I found. To faint means to lose consciousness or to feel dizzy, lightheaded, or weak in the head and body. Although that may be true in medical terms, fainting in Biblical terms resembles something greater, a weakness of the heart and spirit. In the book of Isaiah, God says that we are going to feel faint throughout life; that's a given. When one feels weak, they aren't getting enough nutrients that the body needs. Therefore, they pass out. Well, when a Christian becomes faint, he or she is weak in their spirit and heart. I'm sure no Christian means for this to happen, but if we are not careful, it will result in the consequences of a spirit and heart that are both feeble and frail.

Weak in Spirit or in Heart?

Knowing and admitting one's weakness causes them to gain momentum and try something different to better equip themselves for greatness (whatever that looks like to you). In order for us to have a strong heart and spirit, we have to understand what can make one weak.

1. Not being in God's Word—Being in the Word gives you rejuvenation like no other. I've mentioned how this can affect you in chapter five, "Obedience Isn't Optional."
2. Have little or no communication with God—How often do you pray for your family, your friends, or even yourself? Prayer is the greatest wireless connection we have! Get plugged in and connected with God to grow deeper in your walk with Him.
3. Not involving and investing in your church and ministries within

your community—God made us for community. It's in our DNA. As Christians, we should thrive on being with fellow believers to impact lives for Christ.

4. Desiring the things of the world rather than the God who made them—Giving into fleshly desires and worldly pleasures can lead to a breakable heart and spirit. When you submit yourself to your own desires, the desires of God tend to take a back seat. So, rather than God leading your life, you have become the driver—making for a messy and stressful ride.

Let's pause here for a moment. You are probably saying, *Sierra, you mentioned all of these things before. I already know all of this stuff.* Let me be the first to say congratulations! I'm so proud that you know to do all of these things to help you stay strong in the Lord. However, it is one thing to know to do them but another thing to act upon them.

Remember, it is a sin to know what you ought to do and then not do it.
—James 4:17 (NLT)

Personally, just because you're a Christian doesn't mean your heart and soul are automatically strong. As mentioned previously, both our heart and spirit can be very fragile, in need of mending and TLC every now and again. We, as believers, are to nourish them with the utmost care and attention. In order to achieve this, one has to be determined and dedicated to pleasing the Lord no matter the cost. Spending time in His Word and praying to Him with like-minded believers can affect a person greatly. Remember, having a weak spirit doesn't mean there is no room for improvement. The only place you can go is up. No one can make you change but yourself. So go for it! Take initiative and change your heart and soul for the better, pushing yourself to intimately seek and obey Christ more.

What are some ways you can make your heart and soul strong?

Yoke

Have you never heard? Have you never understood? The Lord is the everlasting God, the Creator of all the earth. He never grows weak or weary. No one can measure the depths of his understanding. He gives power to the weak and strength to the powerless. Even youths will become weak and tired, and young men will fall in exhaustion.

—Isaiah 40:28–30 (NLT)

It is clear that people don't like to struggle and have problems in life. Who does? One bad instance can ruin a perfectly good day, am I right? You get a flat tire and are late for work; maybe you lose your job, or you find out your spouse has an incurable illness that can leave them for months in the hospital, not knowing the outcome. No one likes to have troubles thrown at them. Jesus even said in Isaiah that humans are going to suffer and feel the weight of exhaustion. Maybe not all at once, but sometimes we are going to feel that life's weight of heaviness is burdensome and too much to carry on our own. In the midst of these hardships, where do you turn? Where do you run? Where do you find your strength to keep moving forward? In whom do you trust to guide and help you?

I am reminded of a passage of scripture in Matthew. It says:

Then Jesus said, "Come to me, all of you who are weary and carry heavy burdens, and I will give you rest. Take my yoke upon you. Let me teach you, because I am humble and gentle at heart, and you will find rest for your souls. For my yoke is easy to bear, and the burden I give you is light."
—Matthew 11:28–30 (NLT)

I am going to break these verses down to have a better understanding of what it means to fully rest in God in the midst of life's circumstances.

Verse 1: *Come to me all who are weary and burdened, and I will give you rest.*

Depending on the person, it may take something tragic to completely turn their life upside down. To some people, it may not take much to throw them for a loop. Life's weight differs depending on the individual. Each person is different and unique. What matters is not the heaviness on the person's shoulders but the action it takes to loosen the grip ever so slowly and then release it all at once to ensure peace and relief.

Scripture says all who are weary and burdened, come to Him. Jesus is referring to everyone when He mentions the word all. Nowhere in scripture does it say that certain people will be exempt from having struggles or difficulties while on this earth. No matter how heavy or light your load may be, giving it to the Lord is the best option. God knew that the problems we encounter would be too much for us to handle on our own. Because of this, God has no weight limit. He can handle whatever amount you give Him. You can keep praying and stacking your burdens onto His shoulders, and He will never get tired. That gives me such peace, knowing that my God never grows weary or faint because of my numerous problems. He wants everyone to come to Him with their struggles, knowing that He alone can give us ultimate restoration and sustainment needed to walk through life.

Do you want to keep on carrying life's burdens alone, or do you want to give it to God?

What is the first step to release the heavy grip and weight of your struggle?

Are you able and willing to take that first step? If so, how are you going to make it happen?

Although it is sometimes forced, rest is so good for your mental, physical, spiritual, and emotional health. To be honest, it can be a big challenge for me. I am steadily on the go, with what seems like a numerous amount of stuff to do. However, the Lord commands us all to rest. He wants us to find true rest in Him. It says that not only once but twice in these verses, "I will give you rest." Not "I can" or "I might," but "I will." That is a promise, but only if we accept it.

Though both resting and relaxing can intertwine, they are different in their meaning. Relaxing involves releasing anxieties and tension, while resting requires one to refresh and recover strength. Some people partake in yoga in order to relax. For me, I tend to open my Bible and go into solitude with God by journaling in order to unwind. Now, I am not saying this to brag by any means; I just know how I operate. You may have different methods of relaxing, and that's okay. Whatever the case, truly resting involves refreshing your mind as well as your body.

Likewise, there is also a difference between physical and spiritual rest. Everyone needs physical rest. Getting a good eight hours' worth of sleep a night does a body good for the next day. I know the eight-hour time frame is not necessarily ideal, but whatever your sleep schedule is, hopefully you can be spry for the next day ahead. Regardless of how much sleep you get, do you ever find yourself drained even when you do get a good night's sleep? But when you read the Word, it feels like a recharge and energy boost? I remember my first summer on staff at camp. I probably got around five hours of sleep a night. Going to bed around one in the morning and waking up at six was definitely not what I call fun. I would walk down the staff hill every morning and study for about an hour, either by myself or with campers. Now, that was totally my choice, and I have no regrets. I could have slept in and gotten the rest I needed, but the Lord somehow sustained me. He gave me new energy from reading and studying His Word in the mornings. Although it was hard to get up and study scripture, I encourage you to do so. You will find abundant rest that you may have never felt before.

Working long hours, coming home to a disorganized and messy house, while managing and scheduling time between your spouse and children can get crazy and sometimes monotonous. When our minds and hearts are heavy, it can be hard to find comfort and peace because we are too busy focusing on the problems at hand. Your mind and spirit allow you to listen to God as well as reflect on your life and your circumstances with no distractions or disturbances. Therefore, when we do fully rest in the Lord by digging deep in His Word, we have true peace, knowing that He will restore and strengthen us to conquer whatever life throws our way.

Verse 2: *Take my yoke upon you and learn from me, for I am gentle and humble in heart, and you will find rest for your souls.*

To understand this verse, we have to know what the word yoke means. A yoke is a wooden crosspiece that is fastened over the neck of two animals, like cows or oxen. When farmers used to plow crops, they would hitch up two animals beside each other and place the yoke on them. These animals worked together to do a difficult task, like pulling a heavy load to cultivate a field. The yoke was a device that helped out when one animal stumbled or the weight of the load got too heavy. One animal would be able to rely on the other for support and stability. The same thing can happen with God. When the weight of life's problems gets too much to handle and we can barely stand, the Lord wants us to call on Him for support. To put it bluntly, we will never be able to pull God down with the weight of our load, but He will always be able to hold us up by His divine power and strength. Because God is not a God who crumbles under the weight of sin, we can rely on Him to get through anything this world throws at us.

Truly being honest with ourselves about our problems and challenges can cause us to become better when we self-evaluate. Since God has a gentle and humble heart, He will always support and rescue His people from turmoil. Because of this, as a Christian, I am to mirror the heart of God (see chapter six, "Spotting the Difference"). Jesus was and always will be perfect. The actions of His heart determined His steps. Therefore, I can trust Him to steer me on the right path in this corrupt world by aiming to seek His flawless heart.

Verse 3: *For my yoke is easy and my burden is light.*

The burdens of this world will take us down if we don't rely on the Lord. I've mentioned this time and time again throughout this book. Obstacles will come that are unplanned, and life can turn upside down. However, the Lord is immovable and unshakeable. Even though you may find yourself in a rough patch and on uneven ground, have the Lord be your firm foundation (Matthew 7:24–29).

God's yoke is easy. He wants to support you. He wants to help you. He wants to sustain you. God literally has His arm stretched and His hand out, ready for you to grab. The problem is that we get so fixated on our own independence and our own control that we don't receive God's hand. We want to do it our way or bust. The reality is that God will convict you and fight for you, but He won't fight you. Read that again. God won't fight you. Although His hand is always there, He won't force it upon you. He will let us meander and do things our own way until we come to the realization of our own imperfection, inability, and incoherencies. Once we finally come to terms that we finally need God's help, He receives our hand willingly and without question. He then pulls us up, dusts us off, and gives us renewed strength and the confidence to keep pressing forward.

The Faithfulness of God

Faith is the confidence that what we hope for will actually happen; it gives us assurance about things we cannot see.

—Hebrews 11:1 (NLT)

If you get nothing else from reading this book (although I pray that you do), I want you to cling to this saying: God is faithful. I already talked about why having faith in God is so important, but what about God's faithfulness to us? I mean, if we are faithful and do what He commands, shouldn't He be faithful to us in return?

That's the beauty of it. Although we don't deserve God's faithfulness because we are sinful, God gives us everything if we are faithful to Him. Nowhere in scripture does it say that God owes us _____ (fill in the blank) or God has to do _____ (fill in the blank) for His people. That is quite the contrary. God's faithfulness is not determined by human faithfulness. Meaning, He made us human. Therefore, He knows we are going to mess up and make choices that go against His will. Yet God still loved us enough that He died a gruesome death on a cross. He took the ultimate penalty for our sin. By doing so, this shows that God was faithful to us from the very beginning, before you were even thought of, by wiping our slate clean.

I already stated 1 Peter 5:8–9 in a previous chapter, but I want to unravel the next verse as well.

In His kindness God called you to share in His eternal glory by means of Christ Jesus. So after you have suffered a little while, He will restore, support, and strengthen you, and He will place you on a firm foundation.
—*1 Peter 5:10 (NLT)*

According to this verse, we can interpret suffering for a little while to mean different things. I tend to think of it as a couple of minutes or hours, sometimes even days. Because you are in a battle, I'm sure you want to get out of it soon because you are weary and tired. Trust me, I've been there. Suffering a little while can take a whole new meaning through God's prospective, though. Granted, the Lord never said how long we are going to endure the challenges and struggles we are faced with. Fighting can be hard if you know you are waging a losing battle. However, with God on your side, you have victory no matter what comes your way. If you are a believer, you have already won your battle against the enemy, so giving up the fight is simply not the answer. I can promise you that life is but a vapor (James 4:14). Meaning that the hardships we are faced with will pass. Not necessarily in your timing or the way you want them to (which is hard to understand), but in God's perfect timing. Once you have suffered for a little while, God makes His promise that He will restore your strength, support you, and place you on a firm foundation (your reliance on God and His Word) that is unmovable against the enemy.

When I first came out of my depressive state after high school, it took a while to regain my spiritual mentality as I began to look back and question God. *Why did this happen to me? What did I do to deserve this? Will this come back, and if it does, will I be able to fight against it?* Depression is no joke. As I mentioned previously, it really took a toll on me. I was fighting for my life, mentally, physically, and spiritually. Despite the battle that I was in, I wanted to win with all my being. I didn't want the enemy to get any satisfaction. By God's goodness and faithfulness, I came out of the battle stronger and more reliant on God.

Psalm 23 is a wonderful reminder of God's faithfulness. In these verses, David is singing his praise to God. Being that David faced battles throughout his entire life, he still had a mighty faith in God. These verses state that the Lord leads, renews, guides, and gives rest to His children. Verse 4 is a great reminder that even though we have hard times and pitfalls, the Lord is still faithful.

Now, I don't want to undermine or diminish anyone's struggle. Every person is going to go through hard times while living their life. Therefore, trials will look different for each person. Just remember it is not the battle that defines who you are but the strength and determination to fight to win the battle. I admit that the sun may look bleak in the valley. It is hard to see the light and climb to get back up on the hill. However, David had the right mindset when enduring battles. He said, "Even though I walk through the valley of the shadow of death, I will fear no evil; for You are with me. Your rod and Your staff, they comfort me" (Psalm 23:4, ESV).

Notice the word *through* in this verse. I think this is a faithful promise that if God leads us into a struggle, He will bring us through it as well. If you go through a tunnel, you typically are going in one way and out the other. Basically, if we go through something, we know there is eventually an end. Christians believe that God is faithful and that He will bring us out of whatever He puts in our way. He will provide a way out. Nonbelievers can also have this assurance by receiving the Lord into their heart. Now, that doesn't mean our journeys in life will be easy. God never said they would be. He just said it would be worth it. With that being said, we owe God everything because of His faithfulness to us through it all.

As you live out your life, I strongly encourage you to seek the Lord. He has big plans for you that are unimaginable! I pray that you will live a life worthy of the gift you have been given. My goal here on earth is to seek God and give Him the glory in whatever I set out to do. That doesn't mean my life is perfect. Yet I want to make God known throughout all aspects of my life until He calls me home for eternity. All the twists and turns are all means by which I can glorify God. I pray that you come to see God for who He is. That He is a loving, trusting, caring, and comforting Father who loves you endlessly. I encourage you to shine God's light in the darkness, make Him known in the midst of struggle, and obey and trust Him in the mundane. As our journeys will one day end, and we reach the gates of Heaven,

I pray that both you and I hear the words from Jesus that symbolize a true relationship with Him, "Well done my good and faithful servant."

I have fought the good fight, I have finished the race, and I have remained faithful.

—2 Timothy 4:7 (NLT)

From Emptied To Encouraged

From Emptied To Encouraged

From Emptied To Encouraged

About the Author:

Sierra Rimes, a first-time author, brings her passion for Christ and dedication to guiding the next generation into her writing. Working extensively with children from preschool to youth, Sierra's experiences enhance her insightful perspectives on faith and personal growth. Residing in Florida with her family, she balances her time between her career, studies, and nurturing young minds. Sierra's deep connection to spirituality and commitment to helping others shine through her debut book, *From Emptied to Encouraged*, making it a heartfelt testament to her journey and a guide for readers seeking spiritual and personal enrichment.

www.ingramcontent.com/pod-product-compliance
Lightning Source LLC
LaVergne TN
LVHW041814060526
838201LV00046B/1267